Studies in Mediæval Literature

Edward T. McLaughlin

Alpha Editions

This edition published in 2024

ISBN : 9789364730983

Design and Setting By
Alpha Editions
www.alphaedis.com
Email - info@alphaedis.com

As per information held with us this book is in Public Domain.
This book is a reproduction of an important historical work. Alpha Editions uses the best technology to reproduce historical work in the same manner it was first published to preserve its original nature. Any marks or number seen are left intentionally to preserve its true form.

Contents

INTRODUCTION. .... - 1 -

THE MEDIÆVAL FEELING FOR NATURE. .... - 5 -

ULRICH VON LIECHTENSTEIN. .... - 25 -

NEIDHART VON REUENTHAL, AND HIS BAVARIAN PEASANTS. .... - 47 -

MEIER HELMBRECHT, ... - 65 -

CHILDHOOD IN MEDIÆVAL LITERATURE. .... - 80 -

A MEDIÆVAL WOMAN.[13] .... - 97 -

APPENDIX. .... - 115 -

FOOTNOTES: .... - 119 -

INTRODUCTION.

Edward Tompkins McLaughlin, the writer of the essays contained in this volume, was born at Sharon, Connecticut, on May 28, 1860. He was the son of the Reverend D. D. T. McLaughlin, a graduate of Yale College of the class of 1834. His mother's maiden name was Mary Whittlesey Brownell. She was the daughter of the Reverend Grove L. Brownell, who was settled for many years over the Congregational church of Cromwell, Connecticut. Thus it will be seen that the author of this work belonged on both sides to what Oliver Wendell Holmes has aptly called the Brahman caste of New England.

At the time of his birth his father was pastor of the Congregational church of Sharon, Connecticut, but in 1866 left that place for Morris in the same county. There he remained until 1872 when he gave up parish duties entirely, and retired to Litchfield, which he thenceforward made his permanent home.

With the exception of a short time spent in the Litchfield Academy, the son was fitted for college almost wholly by his father, who was himself a finished scholar in Latin and Greek. He entered Yale in the autumn of 1879, and received the degree of A.B. in 1883. From the very beginning of his university life he was distinguished for his interest in English literature, and during the entire course of it displayed remarkable proficiency in the pursuit of that study. To him, before his graduation, fell the highest honors which the college has to bestow in that department.

After receiving his bachelor's degree he remained another year in New Haven as a graduate student. During that time he devoted himself with increased ardor to the special branches of study in which from the outset he had been interested. In the following year he was made tutor in English. This position he held until 1890, when he was appointed assistant professor of the same subject. At the meeting of the Corporation of the University in May, 1893, he was elected by it to the chair of Rhetoric and Belles-Lettres. Happily married to a wife of congenial tastes, who speedily learned to sympathize with him in the studies which he had made peculiarly his own, he had every reason to expect a long career of usefulness, which would be attended with distinction to himself and would confer distinction upon the institution with which he was connected. But his health had never been vigorous, and in the very summer vacation following his appointment a fever, which came upon him almost without warning, and which seemed at first of slight importance, carried him off after an illness that lasted little more than a week. He died on the 25th of July, 1893, at the age of thirty-three. He lies buried at Litchfield.

Such is a brief sketch of the life of the author of this volume. He had at the time of his death many projects on hand, some partly carried out, some only in contemplation. In 1893 he had edited a volume of selections from English writers under the title of *Literary Criticism for Students*; and since his death a school-edition of Marlowe's *Edward II.*, prepared by him, but left mainly in manuscript, has come from the press. But these were in a measure tasks imposed upon him by the needs of students, and not those undertaken in consequence of his own inclinations. During the last year of his life, however, he had been devoting himself to the preparation for publication of the following essays. He had long been a student of mediæval literature, not merely of that found in the English tongue, but of the much fuller and more varied work that had been produced at an early period on the continent. The writers of France, of Germany, and of Italy, belonging to that period, were in truth so familiar to him that he was sometimes disposed to assume that general acquaintance with them on the part of others which it is the fortune of but few to possess. Some results of this study he now set about putting into permanent form. The first rough draft of the essays here printed had been finished when the fatal illness fell upon him that carried him away.

There is no intention of apologizing either for the matter or the manner of the pieces contained in this volume. They are in no need of it, and in any event what is published must stand or fall upon its own merits. Yet it is the barest justice to the author of these essays to state that not in a single instance do they represent the final form they would have assumed, had he lived to review and revise the first sketches he made. In the case of two of them, which were nearest to the condition in which they were ultimately to appear, evidences of their incompleteness in his own eyes are plainly seen in the manuscripts. Against particular passages and sometimes whole paragraphs there were marginal notes, indicating that the expression was to undergo alteration of various kinds. In several instances a place was marked for the insertion of a transition paragraph which had apparently never been written out, though its character was suggested. These, of course, had all to be disregarded. The condition of things, furthermore, was much worse with the four which had not been so fully completed as the two just mentioned. In the case of these the matter had to be collected and pieced together, at no slight expenditure of time and trouble, from scattered leaves of manuscript, in which it was not always easy to trace out the exact order.

Unfortunately, one essay, intended to be the longest and most important of all, could not be included in this volume. Professor McLaughlin had been for many years an ardent admirer of Dante. To a study of the early life of the great Italian poet he had devoted years of patient research. It was the one subject in which he had the deepest interest, and upon which he had expended the most labor, and he purposed to make the essay dealing with it the principal piece in the work he was preparing. But, as was not unnatural, it was the one essay which needed most the revising hand of its composer. The gaps in it were too numerous and important to justify its insertion in the unfinished condition in which it existed, and this particular piece, upon which the author himself set most store, has been reluctantly laid aside.

But while it is simple justice to state the facts just given, it must not be inferred that these essays, unfinished and even fragmentary as they might have seemed to the writer, will so appear to the reader. Few there will be who will detect that any part of them has failed to receive the full attention to which it is entitled. Nor is it likely, indeed, that the sentiments expressed in these essays would have undergone any material modification, whatever changes might have been made in the manner in which they were set forth. Doubtless some of the points now found in them would have been amplified, others would have been retrenched. Other views again, to which no allusion is made here, would have been introduced. Still, so complete in themselves are the essays in most particulars, that no thought of their incompleteness would have arrested the attention of any save the smallest possible number of readers, had not the condition in which they were left been mentioned in this introduction.

But even had these essays needed much more than they do the revising hand of the author, none the less cordially would they have been received by those who were familiar with his personal presence. Especially is this true of students possessed of literary taste, who have been under his instruction, and it is largely in compliance with their wishes that the publication of this volume was determined upon. For as a teacher Professor McLaughlin, though still young, had attained eminence. He had in particular the rare quality of inspiring those under him with the same zeal for learning and the same love of literature that animated himself.

The teacher of English, it must be confessed, has set before him a task of special difficulty. In the case of other tongues the business of translation, with the verbal and grammatical investigation implied by it, must always constitute the principal part of the work of preparation for the class-room; and the skill and knowledge with which it is performed will of necessity be the main element in testing the proficiency and success of the student. But in the case of English this main part of the usual preparation has been reduced to a minimum. The business has already been done at the pupil's hands. He knows, at least after a fashion, the meaning of the words, even if he does not always comprehend the meaning of the phrase or sentence as a whole in which they are found. The hard task is, therefore, given the teacher of English of starting in his instruction at the point where the teacher of other languages ends. He is, furthermore, to make his subject one of pleasure and profit to that select body of students, who are eager to gain from the pursuit of it all the benefit possible. He is at the same time expected to exact some degree of labor from those who, whether by their own fault or the fault of others, have no interest in this particular subject, if indeed they have interest in any subject whatever. The temptation naturally presents itself to sacrifice the former class to the latter. Especially does this appeal to instructors who are deficient in the literary sense, or who possessing it, lack the ability to arouse it in those under them. The easy process is resorted to of turning the study into one of a purely linguistic character, in which the discussion of words will take the place of the discussion of literature. This is a cheap though convenient method for the teacher to evade the real work he is called upon to perform, and while it may be followed by some incidental advantages, it is almost in the nature of a crime against letters to associate in the minds of young men, at the most impressionable period of their lives, the writings of a great author with a drill that is mainly verbal or philological.

It was the rare fortune of Professor McLaughlin that he solved this problem, presented to every instructor in English, with a felicity that does not fall often to the lot of those engaged in the same occupation. It was not so much in imparting knowledge that his peculiar distinction lay; it was in his success in inspiring interest in the subject and zeal for its prosecution. It is, therefore, more especially to those who have been under his teaching that this little volume is addressed as a memorial of one to whom many will acknowledge is due the first bent their minds received to the study and appreciation of what is best and highest in literature. What its author would have accomplished with his remarkable powers of acquisition and assimilation, had he lived to carry out and perfect plans which he had in contemplation, it is idle to conjecture; and the world, which cares but little for what is actually done in the field in which he was largely working, cannot be expected to concern itself with that which was never more than projected. But there are some to whom the result of his labors, shown in this volume, will prove of interest for what it is; while to those who have known him personally, it will, even in its comparatively imperfect state, furnish a suggestive intimation of what might have been.

T. R. LOUNSBURY

YALE UNIVERSITY,
March 22, 1894.

THE MEDIÆVAL FEELING FOR NATURE.

On the 26th April, 1335, Mt. Ventoux, near Avignon, was the scene of a remarkable occurrence. Petrarch was the hero, and on the evening of that day, while the impression was yet strong upon him, he wrote an account of it to a friend. The incident was nothing less than climbing a mountain for æsthetic gratification. That he cared to do it showed that Petrarch was on the outskirts of mediævalism.

The narrative is so interesting that I may translate a part of it; for the great humanist's letters are inaccessible to general readers. He says that he had thought of climbing the mountain for many years, since he had known the country from early boyhood, and the great mass of rocky cliff, entirely rugged and almost inaccessible, was constantly and everywhere visible. He took with him his brother and two servants. As they were starting on the ascent, they fell in with an aged shepherd, who tried to dissuade them. Fifty years before he had climbed to the summit, moved by a boyish impulse—and he supposed himself the only one who had ever done it; his recollections were full of awe and terror. But the poet pressed on, beguiling the weariness, which at times amounted almost to exhaustion, by moralizing on the labor as a type of spiritual attainments. At the summit of the highest peak, "moved deeply at first by that vast spectacle, and affected by the unusual lightness of the air, I stood as if overwhelmed. I looked, and under my feet I saw the clouds." His thoughts turned to the classical myths, and the history of his beloved Italy. He recalled that ten years before, on that same day, he had left Bologna and his studies. How many changes in his ways. His wrong loves—he loved them no longer, or rather he no longer liked to love them. He thought of his future.

> "Thus rejoicing in what I had gained, regretful of my weakness, and pitying the common instability of human affections, I seemed to forget where I was and why I had come. At last I turned to the occasion of my expedition. The sinking sun and lengthening shadows admonished me that the hour of departure was at hand, and, as if started from sleep, I turned around and looked to the west. The Pyrenees—the eye could not reach so far, but I saw the mountains of Lyonnais distinctly, and the sea by Marseilles; the Rhone, too, was there before me. Observing these closely, now thinking on the things of earth, and again, as if I had done with the body, lifting my mind on high, it occurred to me to take out the copy of St.

Augustine's *Confessions* that I always kept with me; a little volume, but of unlimited value and charm. And I call God to witness that the first words on which I cast mine eyes were these: 'Men go to wonder at the heights of mountains, the ocean floods, rivers' long courses, ocean's immensity, the revolutions of the stars,—and of themselves they have no care!' My brother asked me what was the matter. I bade him not disturb me. I closed the book, angry with myself for not ceasing to admire things of earth, instead of remembering that the human soul is beyond comparison the subject for admiration. Once and again, as I descended, I gazed back, and the lofty summit of the mountain seemed to me scarcely a cubit high, compared with the sublime dignity of man."[1]

In these sentences we find the new life and the old in the same mind. Such an action would have been impossible for a genuine son of the middle ages, but could Petrarch stand on a mountain top to-day, such an outcome of it would be equally impossible. His feeling for nature was intense even to a sense of the charm of ruggedness in hills, as Burckhardt, who refers to this letter in his work on *The Italian Renaissance*, shows by ample quotations; but the intense lover of nature in the nineteenth century, though his ethical sense be as deep as Wordsworth's, finds a different influence in such a scene. Indeed, read in Wordsworth himself, the modern contrast:

"Ocean and earth, the solid frame of earthAnd ocean's liquid mass, in gladness layBeneath him; far and wide the clouds were touched,And in their silent faces could he readUnutterable love. Sound needed none,Nor any voice of joy; his spirit drankThe spectacle; sensation, soul, and form,All melted into him; they swallowed upHis animal being, in them did he live,And by them did he live: they were his life.In such access of mind, in such high hourOf visitation from the living God,Thought was not; in enjoyment it expired.No thanks he breathed, he proffered no request,Rapt into still communion, that transcendsThe imperfect offices of prayer and praise."

How far apart is the piety of the two poets, how different their absorption. This identification of the human mood with Nature, and the spiritual elation that arises from the union, is thoroughly characteristic of the present century. Wordsworth's peculiar beauty, as Hartley Coleridge told Caroline Fox, "consisted in viewing things as amongst them, mixing himself up in everything that he mentions, so that you admire the man in the thing, the involved man." And Hartley's inspired father uttered a great criticism on the modern feeling for nature, when in the *Ode on Dejection* he cried,

"Oh, lady, we receive but what we give, And in our life alone doth nature live."

No literary contemporaries were ever more apart than Wordsworth and Byron, yet *Childe Harold* has the same note:

"I live not in myself, but I become Portion of that around me; and to me High mountains are a feeling.. . . . the soul can flee And with the sky, the peak, the heaving plain Of ocean, or the stars, mingle and not in vain."

We discover the same sentiment, more delicately held, in Keats, as in some of his sayings about flowers, and Shelley, speaking of the longing for a response to one's own nature, says:

> "The discovery of its antitype, this is the invisible and unattainable point to which love tends.... Hence in solitude, or in that state when we are surrounded by human beings, and yet they sympathize not with us, we love the flowers, and the grass, and the waters, and the sky. In the motions of the very leaves of spring, in the blue air, there is found a secret correspondence with our heart, that awakens the spirits to a dance of breathless rapture, and brings tears of mysterious tenderness to the eyes, like the enthusiam of patriotic rapture, or the voice of one beloved singing to you alone."

Yet this spirit, with which our later poetry is almost everywhere touched, "this mysterious analogy between human emotions and the phenomena of the world without us," as von Humboldt expresses it, in its present comprehensiveness is new to literature. To feel for mountains, forests, or the ocean, with mingled awe, love, and ecstasy, seems so natural to us, that we can hardly realize that Gray was striking a novel and significant chord when he wrote at the Grande Chartreuse, "One of the most solemn, the most romantic, and the most astonishing scenes.... Not a precipice, not a torrent, not a cliff, but is pregnant with religion and poetry."

In Petrarch's letter we observe the deficiency in absorbing enthusiasm for the grander forms of nature, as well as his sense of the isolation of such sentiment from true spiritual life. Yet this letter is the most significant indication which we possess from the middle ages of a capacity for enjoying the sublimity of heights. In *Præterita*, Ruskin, while describing his eagerness at the first sight of the Alps, as a boy, has written two or three sentences that we may employ to illustrate the contrast between Petrarch and his predecessors:

> "Till Rousseau's time there had been no 'sentimental' love of nature ... St. Bernard of La Fontaine, looking out to Mont Blanc with his child's eyes, sees above Mont Blanc the Madonna; St. Bernard of Talloires, not the Lake of Annecy, but the dead between Martigny and Aosta. But for me, the Alps and their people were alike beautiful in their snow, and their humanity; and I wanted, neither for them nor myself, sight of any thrones in heaven but the rocks, or of any spirits in heaven but the clouds."

Others, beside the Bernards, men from whose culture and intelligence we should expect fine appreciation, felt nothing august or inspiring in the material world. So far as we have any record, the fourteenth-century laureate was the first of the moderns to climb a mountain for the æsthetic pleasure of the view. Burckhardt's suggestion that this honor belongs to Dante, on the strength of a passage in the fourth canto of the *Purgatory*, is surely not tenable; for the top of Bismantova possessed a citadel in Dante's time to which business may easily have called him. All through the middle ages, the lofty elevations between central Europe and Italy were constantly being crossed. The most cultivated men were going back and forth as couriers on business of the Church, and the political relations, especially between Italy and Germany, kept up a continual stream of travel. Yet one recalls no lines in any mediæval poem that describe or express sensations of the least interest concerning the sights that have bowed the strongest souls of our era, that have been felt by thousands, and put into words by so many poets.

There is, indeed, in the beginning of a passage from a famous scholar, John of Salisbury, an apparent exception to this strange indifference; but a few clauses correct the hasty judgment. Writing from Lombardy, he explained why he could not send a letter from the Great St. Bernard: "I have been on the mount of Jove: on the one hand looking up to the heaven of the mountains; on the other, shuddering at the hell of the valleys; feeling myself so much nearer to heaven that I was more sure that my prayer would be heard." Yet this was due to no rapture of soul, for—"Lord, I said, restore me to my brethren, that they come not into this place of torment." He goes on to specify the perils of ice, precipice, and cold, and nothing disturbs him so much as that his ink was frozen. But there is not a suggestion of anything worth looking at. Even Cæsar, as von Humboldt reminds us, composed a rhetorical treatise while crossing the Alps. But the poet of Vaucluse did climb a mountain for the love of the view, and the very fact that his æsthetic attention was distracted by ethical introspection is an indication of that serious sensibility which was destined to become such an essential element in our feeling for nature; what for every Wordsworthian is summed up in the second mood of *Tintern Abbey*.

This incapacity for appreciating mountainous sublimity involved a blindness to the rugged and picturesque on smaller scales. In minor chords, and in combinations of tone superficially discordant, we have learned to recognize some of nature's richest harmonies; this is one of our marks of development. Closely linked, too, with this first of modern passions for nature, indeed unified with it by the qualities of strength and massiveness, is our feeling for the ocean and great woods.

"There is a pleasure in the pathless woods,There is a rapture on the lonely shore:There is society where none intrudes,By the deep sea, and music in its roar."

Even deeper than the idea of companionship here is the mystical sense of absorption into that physical world which seems the very dwelling-place of the infinite soul, which finds one of its most remarkable manifestations in an intense and almost defiant sensation of human transitoriness and unimportance, and which is frequently blended with very exultation in the reflection that presently we ourselves shall be unified forever with the unconscious life that stretches out before us:

"Rolled round in earth's diurnal courseWith rocks, and stones, and trees."

There is a strange fascination to the modern mind, in presence of the majesties of nature, in this thought of humanity's return to the earth-mother. Innumerable generations have come home to her, as many or more are to be born that they may follow them, and she remains. Perhaps we are never so serenely conscious of self, as in these rare moments when we bear without a pang the thought of losing personal identity. There is something more here than the certainty of at least materialistic immortality, and the impression of infinite repose and beauty.

The projection of our immediate sensation into the long future silence suffuses nature with pantheistic life, until the eager and buoyant thrills of spiritual realization render one grateful to have been permitted to gain such a sensation at what seems the trivial cost of feeling oneself the mere creature of a day. Such a mood as this certainly comes but seldom, but probably every one who has ever experienced any imaginative sensibility to a grand landscape will recall a heightened sensation that is beyond description.[2]

But still stranger than the failure to catch the finer suggestions in the more strenuous forms of nature, is the way in which such sights are ignored. In southern Europe, mountains, storms, rocks, the ocean, are scarcely ever described, even as objects of awe or terror. When in the course of a story they have to be mentioned, the treatment is brief and matter of fact. Heinrich von Veldeke in his famous epic, makes nothing of his necessary introduction of a storm at sea, nor does Gottfried, or indeed any one of this whole period.

Gudrun, that epic of the people which deserves to stand near the more famous *Niebelungen Lied*, treats constantly of the ocean, yet never with any feeling except dread of shipwreck. This poem, however, shows a more northern tone in one or two descriptions of winter, that are at least elaborated. In the scene, for instance, when Herwig and Ortwin arrive at the shore where Hildeburg and Gudrun, almost naked, are washing the clothes for their cruel mistress, we find some realistic touches, such as their trembling before the March wind, in which their hair was streaming as they toiled on the beach, while before them the sea was full of cakes of ice that had broken up under the early spring. In another connection, too, the poet compares something to a thick snowstorm, driven by mountain winds. The sense of fitness in a sympathetic natural environment for the human action, that has been so generally regarded in literature, as by Shakespeare, is indeed occasionally found in mediæval poetry; so in an interesting French romance that relates the trials of a heroine who barely escapes with her life, after the loss of everything dear: "The lady is in the wood and bitterly she wails. She hears the wolves howl, and the screech-owls cry; it lightens terribly, and the thunder is heavy, rain, hail, and wind—'tis wild for a lady all alone."

Exceptions occur now and then. Dante, for example, was impressed by the mountains; no readers of the *Purgatory* need to be reminded of his experience in climbing them. The setting for a mood of unrealized love in one of his lyrics is in winter, among the whitened hills: "He wooed the lady in a lovely grassy meadow, surrounded by lofty hills." But the arbitrary verbal repetitions of the *sestina* modify the original face of the image of the mountains towering about the lover's plain, and the pensive beauty of the whole poem may be connected with an allegory. But I believe that even in Dante we never catch the sense of exultation in the earth's power and majesty.

Our modern feeling for forests is not only at times sombre and oppressive; we also derive a sense of sublime composure from them. This latter sentiment was hardly shared by the mediævals. Dante was only following earlier poets when he located the opening of Hell by a gloomy wood, and his repeated metaphor of life as a forest, "confusing," "gloomy," and "dark," accords with the feeling of his age. He would not have appreciated Chateaubriand. He has left us, however, a rare and interesting reference to the soughing in the pines on the Adriatic, which shows how well his ear could interpret its solemn beauty. The mystical apple-tree, moreover, near the close of the *Purgatory*, whose blossoms are so exquisitely defined, indirectly reminds us how exceptional is a mention of fruit trees in flower. Yet the Provençal, French, and German lyrics constantly begin with the joyousness of spring, and the happy contrast from the season that destroys flowers and foliage. Nothing is more conventional than these nature preludes. Over and over, till we close our books impatiently, we hear reiterations of the charm of spring and summer. There is a slender kind of grace and sincerity that would lend interest to many of these, if they had come down by themselves; but they lie together in books in wearisome uniformity. A dandelion in April is much prettier than the dandelions in June. These preludes are usually in keeping with the love-phrases that follow, cold and imitative. For poets thought and felt in exterior generalities, rather than in detachment and inner consciousness. Their typical landscape may be seen in a passage from Gottfried von Strassburg,—one of Germany's most brilliant poets—where Tristan and Isolde have fled to the forest grotto, in fear of King Mark. The grotto is fitted up luxuriously, in keeping with the temper of the entire poem, but since it is in the wilderness, far away from roads or paths, in a description of its surroundings we might certainly look for a sense of the picturesque. But so far from caring for the wild and rugged, Gottfried does not even like a quiet woodland simplicity.

> "Above the entrance stood three broad lindens, no more; but below, stretching down the slope, were innumerable trees that hid the retreat. On one side was a level stretch where a fountain flowed, a fresh, cool stream, clearer than the sun. Above it, too, stood three beautiful shady lindens that shielded the spring from rain and the sun. Bright blossoms and green grass struggled with each other sweetly on the field. One caught also the delightful songs of birds which sang more delightfully there than anywhere else. Eye and ear each had its pleasure, there was shade and sun, air and breezes soft and pleasing."

He goes on to describe the lovers, in a passage from which I translate the opening:

When they waked and when they slept,Side by side they ever kept.In the morning o'er the dewSoftly to the field they drew,Where, beside the little pool,Flowers and grass were dewy cool.And the cool fields pleased them well,Pleased them, too, their love to tell,Straying idly thro' the glade,Hearing music, as they strayed.Sweetly sang the birds, and thenIn their walk they turned againWhere the cool brook rippled by,Listening to the melody,As it flowed and as it went:Where across the field it bent,There they sat them down to hear,Resting there, its murmur clear.And until the sunshine blazed,In the rivulet they gazed.

These lines are characteristic of Gottfried, even to the lingering verbal repetition, and the picture certainly is pretty, as is the whole account of the lovers' life that follows. Nothing in early German literature comes closer to refined modern sensuousness than Gottfried's best passages; there is a dreamy passion in them, and sometimes they flash. His rich voluptuous strain has more of the poet than the free-liver, and his general tone is curiously modern. It would be a showy phrase to call his *Tristan* the *Don Juan* of the middle ages, for the poems are very dissimilar, yet it is safe to say that we think of Byron as we read him. Contrast these representative poets of the thirteenth and nineteenth centuries in this matter of their feeling for nature. For once among German settings we have a wild scene. But we observe how studiously it is modified into the conventional meadow, with trees in uniform little groups, a grassy field is sprinkled with flowers, there is a spring, and the little stream that escapes from it instead of tumbling down over a rocky bed into a glen, flows across the field. Gottfried mentions mountains and rocks that lie round about, only to point out that they are types of the difficulties and perils to be undergone before reaching love's shrine. The almost inaccessible retreat was necessary as a shelter for the fugitives from Mark's court; the poet has done his best to obliterate the reality. If we turn to Byron, and look for instance at that incomparable passage in which he relates the early love of Juan and Haidee, we observe where he voluntarily places his lovers:

"It was a wild and breaker-beaten coast,With cliffs above and a broad sandy shore;Guarded by shoals and rocks as by a host,With here and there a creek, whose aspect woreA better welcome to the tempest-tost;And rarely ceased the haughty billows' roar."

"And thus they wandered forth, and hand in hand,Over the shining pebbles and the shells,Glided along the smooth and hardened sand,And in the worn and wild receptaclesWorked by the storms, yet worked as it were planned,In hollow halls, with sparry roofs and cells,They turned to rest; and each clasped by an arm,Yielded to the deep twilight's purple charm."

And, to pass over the description of sky, sea, moon, and starlight, that follows, as elements in the nature-setting, notice the scene where Juan is sleeping:

"The lady watched her lover, and that hourOf Love's, and Night's, and Ocean's solitude,O'erflowed her soul with their united power,Amid the barren sand and rocks so rude,She and her wave-worn love had made their bower."

It would be easy to parallel these two situations; the older by no means ends with the middle ages, for Eden's "blissful bower" is no exception in modern poetry before the romantic age: while in our own century counterparts to this conception of untrained and strenuous natural surroundings for even the happiest of emotions will occur to every one.[3] The idle triteness in those inevitable scenes of spring, was manifest to some of the poets themselves. So the Comte de Champagne declares foliage and flowers of no service to poets, except for rhyming and to amuse commonplace people. The great Wolfram himself derides the conventionality of all romance narratives falling in spring and early summer:

Arthur is the man of May;Each event in every lay,Happened or at WhitsuntideOr when the May was blooming wide.

And Uhland cites from the lives of the troubadours the contemporaneous criticism upon a minor poet of the twelfth century, who wrote in the old style about leaves, and flowers, and the song of birds,—nothing of any account. We may recollect that such criticisms go far back of the middle ages: Horace glances at his contemporaries' conventional descriptions of a stream hastening through pleasant fields.

In the widely popular romances of Enid we find illustrations of Welsh, French, and German treatment in the hands of leading authors, and there is one point in the narrative where we may compare their feeling for the natural environment. Readers of Tennyson will recall the passage in the wandering, where, after one of Geraint's struggles with bandits, he comes upon a lad carrying provisions. Chrestien's treatment of the episode is clear and straightforward; the youth and two comrades are taking cheese, cakes, and wine to the count's meadows for the haymakers. The young man notices the travellers' worn appearance, and invites them to sit down "in this fair meadow, under these ironwood trees," to rest and eat.

Hartmann von Aue (whose paraphrase of the French poem is, by the way, far from the merit of his *Iwein*) narrates the incident in the same manner, omitting the poetically specific touches of the haymaking, and the shady spot in the field; but characteristically inserting some courteous concern on the part of the young man, for the comfort of Enid. But if we turn to the *Mabinogion* we come upon something very different:

> "And early in the day they left the wood, and they came to an open country, with meadows on one hand, and mowers mowing the meadows; and there was a river before them, and the horses bent down and drank the water. And they went up out of the river by a lofty steep, and there they met a slender stripling with a satchel about his neck, and they saw that there was something in the satchel, but they knew not what it was. And he had a small blue pitcher in his hand, and a bowl on the mouth of the pitcher."

How charming it is, even to the lovely touch of color. We know here that the unremembered writer saw nature and cared for it as we do. Indeed, this mediæval Welshman satisfies us quite as well as does even Tennyson's transcript:

"So through the green gloom of the wood they passed,And issuing under open heavens beheldA little town with towers, upon a rock:And close beneath, a meadow gemlike chasedIn the brown wild, and mowers mowing in it:And down a rocky pathway from the placeThere came a fair-hair'd youth, that in his handBare victual for the mowers."

There we have a simplicity treated with Tennysonian artifice, which "victual" does not succeed in correcting; beautiful in its way, though its way is perhaps not so fine as the prose. Yet we notice the modern spirit in the appreciation of the "brown wild" as well as the meadow, and out of the more general and evasive "steep" is developed the picturesque "rocky pathway."

Except for the interest in establishing these forms of nature-appreciation from such older and more original sources, we might have satisfied ourselves with illustrations of them from Chaucer's early poems, where his descriptions are almost wholly derivative. His feeling for "the smale, softe, swote gras," that was sweetly embroidered with flowers; the earth's joyous oblivion of the cold, in her enthusiasm of May; his constant delight in the "smale foules," and the like, are purely conventional, though the unction with which he writes shows his real enjoyment. There are touches in Chaucer, however, that we miss in his romance predecessors, such as his eye for delicate effects—most interesting as marking the growth of accurate observation and sensitive rendering, like the description of twilight in *Troylus and Creyseyde*, when

"White thynges wexen dymme and donneFor lakke of lyght,"

or the graceful illustration in the same poem of a sudden troubling of one's mood:

"But right as when the sonne shyneth brighteIn March that chaungeth ofte tyme his face,And that a cloude is put with wynde to flyght,Which overspret the sonne, as for a space,A cloudy thought gan through his soule pace."

Such a touch makes us feel how modern he is. Yet he does not love the picturesque. Under the influence of a Breton lay, he writes in the loveliest of all his tales, of the rugged sea-coast on whose high bank Dorigen and her friends used to walk (since "stood hire castel faste by the see") and look down upon "the grisly rokkes blake," which, in her apprehension for her lord's safe return, she would call "these grisly, feendly rokkes blake." But we feel that even had Arviragus been at her side she would never have regarded the coast as we should regard it. Still we observe the advance in observation and literary expression. In the *Knight's Tale*, the wild picturesque is employed again to connote the terrible, but no poet, from Statius to Boccaccio, his guides in the passage, had written such lines as his setting for the temple of the God of War:

"First on the wal was peynted a forestIn which there dwelleth neither man nor best,With knotty, knarry, bareyne trees oldeOf stubbes sharpe and hidous to biholde,In which ther ran a rumbel and a swough,As though a storm sholde bresten every bough."

Nothing even in *Childe Roland* sketches desolating natural effects with more power. Yet Chaucer had a superior, in the sympathetic eye and adequate expression for the stern and stormy phases of nature, in a countryman of whom perhaps he never heard. We do not know the name of the author of *Sir Gawayn and the Grene Knyght*. But the poem marks on the whole the noblest conception in our literature before Spenser. It possesses moral dignity, romantic interest, simplicity, and directness, united with deep seriousness of style, creative imagination in dealing both with character and with nature. Chaucer wrote nothing so spiritual, though much of course more artistic and poetically valuable. In regard to this one matter of the interpretation of nature, it would be difficult to point out passages in the whole range of mediæval literature so fine and so remarkable as such descriptions as follow, of the northern winter scenes through which Gawayn passed on his weird mission.

A forest full deep, and wild to a wonder,High hills on each side, and crowded woods under,Of oaks hoar and huge, a hundred together.The hazel and hawthorne were grown altogetherEverywhere coated by moss ragged, rough;Many birds on bare branches, unhappy enough;That piteously piped there, for pain of the cold.

Wondrous fair was the earth, for the frost lay thereby;On the mist ruddy gleams the sun cast, as on highHe coasted full clearly the clouds of the sky.

They beat along banks where the branches are bare,They climbed along cliffs where clingeth the cold,The clouds yet held up, but 'twas ugly beneath.Mist lowered on the moor, dissolved on the mountains.Each hill had a hat, a huge misty cloak.Brooks boiling and breaking dashed on the banks,Shattered brightly on shore.

That is what we find in the North, and such English feeling for the sublime is nothing new; it goes far back beyond these lines into the generations that seem misty as the air which their poets are wont to describe. Mr. Stopford Brooke's recent volume on Anglo-Saxon poetry makes it unnecessary to enter into the subject of old England's eye and ear for nature. Its accounts of the sympathy for the bold and fierce bear out what one might guess without knowledge—that the stern northern climate and familiarity with ocean life found large poetical expression. Luxury, southern artifice of sentiment and literary manner, had not invaded the rugged men of the North; they delight in describing elemental conflicts, and sometimes with studied elaboration. But if the pictures of the German and French poets are uniform in their mildness, those of these Anglo-Saxons are marked by their stormy aspect. We exchange spring for winter.

The same contrast holds true when we take up the Scandinavian poets; they show much feeling and power, but little susceptibility to the beauty of gentleness and grace. Mr. Brooke has remarked upon a similarity between the *Tempest* of Cynewulf and Shelley's *Ode to the West Wind*. A closer parallel may be observed in the *Lines Among the Euganean Hills* and the so-called Helgi poet; where we find a curiously identical image of rooks and hawks flying into the early morning with wings sparkling from the mists through which they have passed. The Norse poems are fond of screaming eagles, and ravens on the high branches.

That weird northern imagination too has vivid pictures, as the shields of the night-warriors shining in the waning moon. Nature also occasionally speaks to their personal moods, both by harmony and contrast. A poet's boat is swept fiercely by the tempest, as he dies with thoughts of his "linen-clad lady" in his heart. Another watches the sea dashing against the steep cliff, and thinks of his far-away love, in the control of his rival. Like the early English, they feel exultation in sea and storm. They know them intimately and their descriptions are spirited and faithful. They love them, but they love fiercely, terribly, as they do their women. Yet even as in their human passions, there are tranquillities. "They rode their steeds through dewy dales and dusky glens: the air, a sea of mist, shook as they passed by." We linger behind the storming horsemen for a moment, to look back as the silence steals in again through those dusky glens.

But to return to what is our real subject, the sentiment for nature in what we may term the polite literatures of mediævalism.

The reason for their feeling about winter is summed up in one of the Latin student songs, "the cold icy harshness of winter, its fierceness, and dull, miserable inactivity." It kept them within, when their interests and concerns were so mainly out-of-door. The poets are for ever singing in praise of spring, not so much because they loved it for itself, as because it brought them a life that was gay and easy. They seldom introduce touches of appreciation in their descriptions of the wintry season. Snow may have appeared lovely to them, but we observe Dante as doing something singular when he compares the talking of ladies, which was mingled with sighs and tears, to raindrops interspersed with beautiful snowflakes (*cp. Inf.*, 14, 30; 24, 5), and one of the most memorable lines in his friend Guido Cavalcanti's poems is the one which mentions the dreamy sinking down of snow, falling when the air is windless. The old-time gentlemen apparently hugged the fire and drank of "their bugle-horn the wyn," and ate "brawn of the tusked swyn," when winter came, instead of watching the snow, through their little windows.

There are many phases of nature which it seems to us impossible not to notice and enjoy, of which we seldom find a trace. We should expect them in the large body of lyrical verse, and still more in the copious romance literature, which corresponds to the modern novel, both in incident and in the invitation to bits of passing local color. Clouds, for instance, aside from their glory of line and mass, and the grace and loveliness of their lighter forms, are curious and oddly suggestive, as Antony reminds Eros, and they are constantly before the eye; yet let any reader of mediæval poetry recall how imperceptible a part they play in it, even as plain facts of description. A line in one of the Latin songs expresses the feeling: their thought of clouds is, how delightful not to see them. Moonlight, too, is seldom dwelt on as poetical; the most romantic touch that comes to my mind in connection with it, is in Chrestien de Troyes, where it shines over the reconciliation of estranged lovers. Just as we find little notice of sunrise, sunset, clouds, and moon, we find little feeling for the stars. They are mentioned occasionally in a facile way, though scarcely ever with manifest sentiment. There are two or three passages, however, in *Aucassin et Nicolette*, that show the daintiest sort of sentiment for moonlight and stars. Here, for instance, where the lovers are confined for the sake of thwarting their love:

> "'Twas in summer time, in the month of May, when the days are warm, long, and clear and the nights calm and cloudless. Nicolette was lying one night in her bed, and she saw the moon clearly shining through a window, and she heard the nightingale singing in the garden and she thought of Aucassin her lover, whom she loved so much."

So making a rope of the bedclothes she lets herself down into the garden.

> "Then she caught her gown by one hand in front and by the other behind, and tucked it up on account of the dew which she saw was heavy on the grass, and she went down through the garden.... And the daisy-blossoms that she broke with the toes of her feet, that lay over on the small of her foot, were even black, by her feet and legs, so very white was the dear little girl. Along the streets she passed in the shadow, for the moon shone very clear, and she went on till she came to the tower where her lover was."

And again when the lover is in pursuit of her, after she had built herself a lodge in what she thought a safe retreat; he does not know where she is, and his thoughts are so absorbed that he falls and puts out his shoulder, and then creeps into her vacant shelter:

> "And he looked through a break in the lodge and saw the stars in the sky, and he saw one brighter than the rest, and he began to say:

'Pretty little star, I seeWhere the moon is leading thee.Nicolette is with thee there,My darling with the golden hair;God would have her, I believe,To make beautiful the eve.'"

Yet even here there is nothing of the deeper sensibility to midnight sky, common alike to ancient and modern seriousness. Yet we find notes also of this. It is hard, for example, to think of giving up the genuineness of Dante's letter refusing to return to Florence, if only for the rare touch of everywhere seeing the sun and the stars (*nonne solis astrorumque specula ubique conspiciam?*), that bears out such evidences as the last word of each of the divine canticles and other fine proofs that he felt the high wonder and peace of the stars at night. Who can doubt that he did—that every deep nature always has? Yet the poetical evidence for it is curiously scanty throughout these centuries. It is a surprise to come upon such an exclamation as this of Freidank's: "The constellations sweep through heaven as if they were alive,—sun, moon, the bright stars,—there is nothing so wonderful!"

Indeed, I can recall no writer to whom the material world seems to suggest such inner sensations as he who called himself Freidank, the German free-thinker. He was not much of a poet, so far as his verses go, but his soul knew life as mystery. He also made one of the band of reformers three centuries before Luther. He saw the corruption of the Church, yet he revered the sacred institution; in spite of his faith, he was a Christian rationalist. Some of his sentences almost startle us, as words before their season: "If the Pope can forgive sins by indulgence, without repentance, people ought to stone him if he allows any one to go to hell." "God is constantly shaping new souls, which he gives to men—to be lost. How does the soul deserve God's wrath before it is born?" He is haunted by the secret of life: "How is the soul made? No one tells me that. If all souls could be in a hand, none could see or grasp their glory." "Earth and heaven are full of the Godhead. Hell would be empty, were God not there." "Whatever the sun touches, the sunlight keeps pure. However the priest may be, the mass is still pure. The mass and the sunshine will always be pure." "I never cease wondering how the soul is made. Whence it came, and whither it fares—the path is hidden. Nay, I know not who I am myself.[4] Lord God, grant me that I may know thee, and also myself." So when Freidank hears the roar of the wind, its invisible might reminds his skepticism that the soul may well be great, though none can see it: while he watches the wide mist which no hand can seize upon, a symbolism of the soul comes to him again. He is oppressed by the restless energy of being: "Our hearts beat unceasingly, our breaths are seldom still:—and then, our thoughts and dreams!" As he rides through spring, he observes the infinite diversity of nature:

Many hundred flowers,Alike none ever grew;Mark it well, no leaf of greenIs just another's hue.

"Many a man looks out at the stars, and tells what wonders take place there. Let him tell me now (something closer at hand), what is the weed in the garden. If he tells me that truly, I shall be more ready to believe the other." It is the germ of Tennyson's *Flower in the Crannied Wall*. Nature's commonplaces hold the heavenly mystery in a common bond with their own. Such subtle blendings of the outward and inward vision could come only from a refined and pensive spirit—such as his who sums up thus the discipline of life: "Many a time the lips must smile when the heart weeps."

One of the marked deficiencies of all these descriptions of nature is in the indefiniteness of the terms employed. In minute accuracy, Dante, to be sure, is one of the world's greatest masters; but elsewhere it is rarely that we come upon anything concrete or specific. It is not until centuries later, indeed, that, so far as nature goes, we find habitual composition "with the eye upon the object," but, as it seems, most mediæval poets never carried their observation beyond the barest general impressions. We do not expect Tennyson's "More black than ashbuds in the front of March," or Browning's eye for the fact that when "the leaf-buds on the vine are woolly," the red is about to turn gray. The outer world's "open secret" is not open enough to make us demand minute attention. But it is surprising that they did not more frequently record easy impressions, and in their inventions introduce definite details. The poetical effect of even apparently prosaic precision is at times imaginative, but the art of this was kept for the later romanticists.

There is a lyric, however (belonging, I believe, to the twelfth century), by a poet of northern France, and written as a satire on the love-romance literature of the age, which contains one or two happy instances of just this missing trait. So charming it is in itself that I have translated it as a whole, though it belongs to an essay on the lyrical romances, instead of on nature. What a light touch the unknown writer shows, what dainty fancy! Sir Thopas is hardly a parallel to this blending of poetry with humor, a humor too gracious to be derisive, whose genial satire sparkles and dances to meet its sister wave of sentiment and beauty, till they ripple together, and each seems to have absorbed the other. The opening stanza is the poet's introduction of himself, and from the olive we may draw an inference respecting his local associations:

Will ye attend me, while I singA song of love,—a pretty thing,Not made on farms:—Nay, by a gentle knight 'twas madeWho lay beneath an olive's shadeIn his love's arms.

1.

A linen undergown she wore,And a white ermine mantle, o'erA silken coat;With flowers of May to keep her feet,And round her ankles leggings neat,From lands remote.

2.

Her girdle was of leafage green;Spring foliage, with a fringing sheenOf gold above;And underneath a love-purse hung,By bloomy pendants featly strung,A gift of love.

3.

Upon a mule the lady rode,The which with silver shoes was shode;Saddle gold-red;And behind rose-bushes threeShe had set up a canopyTo shield her head.

4.

As so she passed adown the meads,A gentle childe in knightly weedsCried: "Fair one, wait!What region is thy heritance?"And she replied: "I am of France,Of high estate.

5.

"My father is the nightingale,Who high within the bosky pale,On branches sings;My mother's the canary; sheSings on the high banks where the seaIts salt spray flings."

6.

"Fair lady, excellent thy birth;Thou comest from the chief of earth,Of high estate:Ah, God our Father, that to meThou hadst been given, fair ladye,My wedded mate!"

Everything here is definite and concrete, and how delightful the picture all is. Such plastic art as the "rose-bushes three" is not unworthy of the great modern poets of whom its magic and romantic definiteness reminds us,— as the "five miles meandering of Alph, the sacred river," or the "kisses four" with which the pale loiterer shut the eyes of La Belle Dame sans Merci. The description of the nightingale on its high branches, too, is a noticeably accurate touch, as we compare it, for example, with Coleridge's nightingale descriptions.

The explanation for the usual vague and indefinite description is not found in saying that they could not describe minutely. We meet with abundant details of such material interests as embroideries or armor. There is artistic emotion in Villehardouin's account of the glorious sight of Constantinople, as it rose before the crusaders, just as distinctly as in Lord Byron's letter. But, to their simple eyes, nature not only failed to suggest associated fancies, like Shakespeare's

"Wrinkled pebbles in the brook,"

or Wordsworth's ash,

"A soft eye-music of slow waving boughs,"

but they see natural objects as units, without lingering upon their parts. When we find, for example, a line that marks the jerky flight of a swallow, we are surprised at the specific touch; we look almost in vain for such landscape details as the colors of autumn. Neidhart von Reuenthal is marking his originality, when he speaks of the red tree-tops, falling down yellow.

The want of observation and the shallow sympathy with nature shown by most poets before Dante are much more surprising than their preference for placid effects. It is unusual, for instance, to meet such a suggestive note of association as in the stanza by the Frenchman Gaces Brulles:

The birds of my own landIn Brittany I hear,And seem to understandThe distant in the near;In sweet Champagne I stand,No longer here.

This paraphrase, indeed, is unworthy of the charming simplicity of the original. Surely, when Matthew Arnold made his sweeping characterization of mediæval poetry as grotesque, he forgot what a straightforward evolution of narrative or of quiet sentiment, and what a transparent expression, we find in some of these minor poets. They are as direct and unadorned, as they are graceful. It is almost impossible to translate them without substituting for the fresh and delicate touch, some metaphysical warping of the idea, or some rhetorical consciousness in words. What for instance could be more elegantly remote from the grotesque than this literal translation of Brulles' expression of his sensibility to the song-birds of his home: "The birds of my country I have heard in Brittany; by their song I know well that in sweet Champagne I heard them of old."

We may sum up these outline statements to this effect.

The northern poets described storm, winter, the ocean, and kindred subjects, with considerable force and fulness. In the cultivated literatures to the south, natural description was mainly confined to the agreeable forms of beauty; the grand, awesome, and inspiring were scarcely felt, and the literal fact of their physical expression was hardly ever noticed. The exterior world was not made a subject of close observation, nor was its poetic availability realized as a setting for action, or as an interpreter of emotion.The people of the north, through being habituated to severer weather, not merely as a fact of climate, but from their rougher, less politely organized habits of living, [we should especially observe their activity on the sea,] regarded the violent seasons and aspects of nature with the sympathetic acquiescence of custom. Moreover, this influence tended to develop sturdier and more rugged character, race-temperament obviously being in part a geographical result, which acts with the forces of social organization, especially those that affect the moral qualities, such as rude or luxurious living. This vigorous character was more susceptible to impressions of native power, as well as from association more interested in recalling them. Accordingly, we find the early northern poetry an anticipation of the seriousness of modern English literature, and, as well, of its unequalled recognition of physical symbolisms of the sublime. Where the northern force blended with more southern lightness and elegance, as it did in the *Mabinogion*, we find a deeper poetic sentiment; where it coincides with moral earnestness, we find such nature sensation as in the poetry of *Sir Gawayn*. But the literature of the Germans and their romance originals, aim at courtly levities; they artificialize sentiment and thought, as well as manner. The deeper and more spiritually sympathetic minds did not as a rule devote themselves to *belles-lettres*. The Church drew them into her sober service, and even though they wrote, the close theological faith was not favorable to their poetic expansion. Most of all, there was but little individualism, and any artistic sensation of our modern complex inner consciousness was still crude, even when it existed at all.

One point, however, should be observed in any inquiry into the reasons for the inadequateness of these ages' feeling for nature; that many latent sympathies may never have found a voice. Many through the centuries before our later ease of publication, may have felt the modern sensations, without ever thinking of putting them into words. In any new movement, of art as of practice, a great leader of expression is needed. Men are sheep to their leaders in various admirations, and many genuine æsthetic tastes are acquired, through stages of more or less unconscious imitation. Browning puts this in an acute sentence where Fra Lippo Lippi explains his usefulness as a painter:

" . . . We're made so that we love,First when we see them painted, things we have passedPerhaps a hundred times, nor cared to see."There were few new departures, there was little originality, in the methods of mediæval literature. Descriptions of the physical world as a field of power and sublimity would have fallen dead on the ears of a public who had never dreamed that storm and cliffs were beautiful. What if Wordsworth had tried to support himself and win fame by singing at castles? Nor is it easy, though the taste has been established, to describe a sunset, or the sublimity of the Alps. We say to each other "How beautiful!" "How grand!" seldom more. Rare imagination and the tact of genius are necessary to tell what we really need to show. The sense of physical sublimity is complex. Its distinctive element is moral or spiritual emotion. For a full delineation it requires a more subtle, verbal repertory than those popular poets usually possessed. Yet these modifications no longer apply when we come to Dante, and superior as his interpretations are to his predecessors' we miss even in him, as we miss in the great poets for four hundred years afterwards, appreciation of the material world's sublimity.

Macaulay and others have said that it was not until man had become the master of nature that he learned to love its stern and violent aspects. But thunder storms, for example, are as dangerous now as they ever were, at least to a traveller. Still, Byron wrote of them with raptures amid the Pindus mountains as his predecessors did not.

Winter was scarcely colder or bleaker for mediæval poets than for Scottish peasants a century ago, yet Burns would sing as they could not:

"E'en winter bleak has charms for me,When winds rave through the naked tree."Others have accounted for this change by the era of science, with its close scrutiny of the world, and its enthusiasm for physical knowledge. But the scientist masters the world as a reality where the poet sees it as a symbol. The two modern tendencies may be the result of a common cause—that recognition of complexity, and disposition to observe, which is a main fact in man's expansion.

A better explanation may be found, I believe, in modern refinement and ethical sensitiveness.

Side by side with the new appreciation of nature may be observed a steady growth in sensibility. Our modern moods of inward contemplation—we are famous for them—our modern zeal for humanity down to its lowest grades; nay, even our tenderness for the brutes, have been distinguishing marks of the poet guides under whom we have learned to appreciate our new physical symbolisms of human emotion. Modern melancholy, as well, a melancholy more subtle and thoughtful, more poetical too, than that of mediævalism, has touched men with its pensive fascination. Philosophical pantheism such as Wordsworth's or Tennyson's, feels deity in nature; the new Christianity incarnates divinity in universal man. Man is more than he used to be, his moods are deeper, his thought freer. He seeks more ardently than of old, because with less constraint, the mystery in whom he lives and moves and has his being. He no longer quails before the majesty and awe of its forever elusive presence. For he knows that though he cannot find it, it enfolds him with love and beauty, it cries back to his passion and pain in winter and storm; from the solemn mountains it reminds him of himself, an unconquerable partner of its own eternity.

ULRICH VON LIECHTENSTEIN.

THE MEMOIRS OF AN OLD GERMAN GALLANT.

Any one who has read Freytag's excellent studies of German social life will recall a curious illustration in his first volume of the lawless violence of thirteenth-century knighthood, in the imprisonment of Ulrich von Liechtenstein by his liegeman Pilgerin. The account not only proves the author's point, but it goes on to suggest a good deal besides. For the victim's unsophisticated and plaintive manner under his misfortune, the fashion in which he relates what he suffered, his allusions to his own life and character, and most of all to the consolations of his love, are all stimulating to one's curiosity about the writer. When we go to the mediæval shelves of a German library we find this curiosity satisfied in a long poem by the unfortunate Ulrich, and immediately we are in that chivalric age which wins most of its romantic lustre from its devotion to womanhood.

If our guesses at a truth beneath the stories of widowed ladies rescued from bandits of the forest and recreant knights, or of lovely ladies rescued from worse than death by the capture of castles through the prowess of generous champions—stories which every one knows and incredulously likes—send us to a study of the times when they were composed, we find that the age, when stripped of romantic embellishments, in its actual life felt a sentiment for women unequalled by earlier times. We wonder what caused it. Can it have been the increase in the culture of the Virgin, that beautiful and beneficent phase of mediæval religion? In its larger development, this appears rather the parallel expression of some common influence, these adorations of the divine and human conceptions of woman seeming to be mutually impulsive, and drawn alike from some undetermined tendency of social and spiritual refinement. Or was it the Crusades? For a German essayist has suggested that we may count this increase of sentimentalism among their many influences upon western Europe; the beauty of the women and the more luxurious habits of the East, its more effeminate emotionalism, finding impressionable subjects in the hearts of those stranger knights lying, wakeful for home, beneath southern stars. Perhaps the conjecture is equally reasonable that the influence came from French poets who, as they travelled with the early Christian armies, caught such suggestions from snatches of oriental poetry. Yet it seems more natural to regard the growth of knightly sentiment toward ladies as the more delicate manifestation of a spontaneous increase of social personality, which was stimulated by that general motion in mind and heart which we observe in the progress of chivalric and crusadal life, and based, as we must not forget, upon that Teutonic character, whose ancient deference to woman is recorded by Tacitus side by side with his account of knighting youthful soldiers with spear and shield.

But, to waive the question of its origin, we find its main expression in the old society, in that protracted and conventional wooing which, we should remember, was not usually directed toward marriage. As gentlemen grew hyperbolical and fantastic in their professions of regard and devotion, feminine coquettishness and love of admiration naturally became fastidious and exacting. Ladies grew arbitrary and capricious, and began to demand substantial proofs of their lovers' concern for them. It became a trait of elegant culture for a lady to pose as inexorable, while still retaining her control over the wooer; while he, complaisant to the sentimental fashion, sighed in a cheerful melancholy, obeyed, adored, and waited. The mistress set tasks, often no trifles, which the loyal subject must perform—hard feats of arms, long and perilous journeys, abnegations of pride or comfort. When these were accomplished, he sometimes returned to receive a new test, involving a continued delay of his reward. These mediæval ladies were as pitiless as the mystic spiritual dictatress of Browning's *Numpholeptos*, to their devotees:

"Seeking loveAt end of toil, and finding calm aboveTheir passion, the old statuesque regard."

In the fourteenth century something of this romantic tyranny survived. We find Chaucer, for instance, in one of his early poems, mentioning in praise of his heroine that she did not impose dangerous expeditions to distant countries, or extravagant exploits upon her lover:

"And saye, 'Sir, be now ryght wareThat I may of you here seynWorshippe, or that ye come agayn.'"

Extended probations, courtships long enough to satisfy Ruskin, were an established convention. Wolfram von Eschenbach, in the seventh book of *Parzival*, represents Obie as indignantly telling her royal lover, who has asked her to marry him after what seems to him a reasonable love-making, that if he had spent his days for five years, in hard service, under full armor, with distinction, and she had then said "Yes" to his desire, she would be yielding too soon.

Jane Austen, in the novel to which Trollope gave the palm of English fiction before *Henry Esmond*, has expressed in Mr. Collins's address to Elizabeth exactly the notion of the significance in a rejection, held by well-bred gentlemen six centuries earlier:

> "'I am not now to learn,' replied Mr. Collins, with a formal wave of the hand, 'that it is usual with young ladies to reject the addresses of the man whom they secretly mean to accept, when he first applies for their favor; and that sometimes the refusal is repeated a second or even a third time. I am therefore by no means discouraged by what you have just said, and shall hope to lead you to the altar ere long.'"

But these exercises, as was suggested, were not usually directed toward the altar. A characteristic of the age is the relation, less or more sentimental, between a married knight and a lady not his wife; a relation rather expected of the former, and countenanced in the latter. This peculiar dual system of domestic and knightly love may be ascribed to various influences, such as the prosaic influence of early and dowered marriages, subject to parental arrangement, or the feudal life which for considerable periods kept gentlemen away from their own homes in residence in the larger castles, or the idleness of such a society, or again the popularity of love-lyrics and romance-recitals, which would tend to sentimentalize their audience. At any rate, it came to be a fashionable idea that the highest love was independent of marriage, and the most poetically inclined,—the troubadours and the minnesingers—were famous for their impassioned and submissive service of married ladies. It is from these poets' accounts of their own love-trials that we learn most about this phase of mediævalism, and in their contented sufferings we see once more that the joy of all romantic love is in the lover.

Although there is danger of generalizing too widely from literary indications, we may believe that chivalric society was appreciably marked by formal amatory disciplines. Was it all for nothing these ceremonial disciplines? Can it be that these Don Quixote prototypes, who trifled away their frivolous days in lady-worship so trivial, did anything to help the Prince to take Cinderella from the ashes? The ashes, then the fairy coach; first the drudge, then the sentimental plaything, then at last the friend. In those days, as perhaps always, the lover objectified himself in his love, to the extent of finding in her his own *ideal feminine*. The very fact that this self, which he probably called into conscious life only as he created it in another, represented the most refined side of his thought, as is shown in the old poets' recurrent epithets of "constant, chaste, good," etc., made the devotion a refining and dignifying experience, especially for the days when men and women had less in common than they have now. These lady-services, where the lover often was denied intimacy for a considerable time, kept up the illusion which the devotee himself may have half felt was sentimental and artificial. We may reply to little Peterkin that some good did come of it at last, even for the more commonplace of these servants of abstract womanhood. Even if the "visionary gleam" left no permanent illumination, the men were better for seeing it brightening through their darkness now and then. At its best, lady-loving gave the mediæval knights consideration for women and a measure of gentleness. If it only stimulated some to fight hard, they would have fought anyway, and the motive was a shade less brutal than a directly selfish one.

But such an eccentric social idea, especially when the poetic exhilaration of its earlier hours has passed by, was sure to bring out extravagant sentimentalists, whose romantic sensibility with no check from practical judgment, ran wild steeplechases of nonsense. Such, for example, was the Provençal poet, Peter Vidal, one of the most famous troubadours, who carried his romantic infatuations so far that he became crack-brained. The name of one of his ladies was Lupa, Mistress Wolf; and if he had contented himself with assuming a wolfish device for his coat-of-arms, as he did, and having himself called Mr. Wolf, he would have done nothing very peculiar, for that age. But it occurred to him that it would be a graceful symbol to wear a wolf's skin, and after he had procured one which quite covered him, he got down on all-fours, and trotted through the street; and all went charmingly until one day, while he was exhibiting himself in this fashion about his lady's estate, a pack of dogs was deceived by the metaphor, and the allegorical lover was badly bitten before rescue arrived.

But the most detailed example of mediæval gallantry is that presented in the work already mentioned, the autobiography of the thirteenth-century minnesinger, Ulrich von Liechtenstein. The poem is a prolix narrative of his amatory religion, extending through some sixteen thousand lines, and containing a large number of lyrics composed in the wooing of two ladies to whom he consecrated his literary and romantic life. We utterly tire of the commonplaces in which he praises them. We reflect that not a single specific incident is ever introduced to illustrate the inner character of either; the descriptions have no color, except in the heartlessness of the first beloved, whose virtue and humor alike Ulrich apparently misses. Yet this presumably undesigned caricature of the more poetic twelfth-century chivalric love gives important suggestions of the times, and Ulrich himself is a knight and a poet worth knowing.

The impression that his romance makes upon a modern reader is something like that of a beetle hovering above a lily. He played zany to the gentlemen of an early generation who had amused their leisurely lives by courtly lady-service; as he emulated their feats of sentimental gallantry, he stumbled and fell. The odd thing is that after each fall he called for his tables: "Meet it is I set it down." Undoubtedly many marvelled and admired, as they looked on: others marvelled and laughed. Perhaps he mistook the laughter for applause. It may be that the sound was lost in the applause of his own simple-minded complacency. But yet, though this gallant was born to a foolish horoscope, his life gained a good fortune denied multitudes who lived sensibly,—he saw the stars of his destiny, and he loved them. Their combination caused a silly career, yet individually they were admirable,—simplicity of nature, theoretical reverence for womanhood, patient love, regard for stately old usages. If defective eyesight makes a man fancy a burdock a rosebush, and if he tends and cherishes the absurd idealization,—at least, the man has a sentiment for roses.

The earliest fact which Ulrich has confided to us, is that in his childhood he used to ride about on sticks, in imitation of the knights, and while in that simple age he noticed that the poetry which people read, and the conversation of wise men which he overheard, kept declaring that no one could become a worthy man without serving unwaveringly good ladies, and that "no one was right happy unless he loved as dearly as his own life some one whose virtue made her fitly called a woman." Whereupon, he thought in his simplicity that since pure sweet women so ennoble men's lives, he, whatever happened, would always serve ladies. In such thoughts he grew up until his twelfth year, when he began a four or five years' term as page to a lady who was good, chaste, and gentle, complete in virtues, beautiful, and of high rank. She was destined to give Ulrich much trouble, and the lover's sweet solicitude began at once, as he started in his teens. For his constant attention found nothing in her but what was good and charming, and he feared—this boy of thirteen—that she might not care for him. His ups and downs of fortune are reported for us in the popular mediæval form (used for example by Map, and one as late as by Villon), of a dialogue between his heart and his body. Heart is hopeful, but Body has the better wit. Yet even if she is too high-born to notice him, he will always serve her late and early, and in the interim between his childish page-waiting, and the bold knighthood to be his when he grows up, he gathers pretty summer flowers, and carries them to her. When she took them in her white hand, he was happy.

As the time came near for him to leave her household, the youth grew emotional: when at table water was poured over those lovely white hands, he transformed her finger-glass into a tumbler. A German dry-as-dust has laughed at Ulrich for this.

But the tender little Teutonic blossom could unfold its youth no longer in the sunshine of its lady-desire. The stern father appeared, and transferred the lover, his "grief showing well the power of love," to the service of an Austrian Margrave. "My body departed, but my heart remained"; and Ulrich pauses for a moment to point out the strangeness of the paradox. "Whenever I rode or walked, my heart never left her; it saw her at all times, night and day."

His new master was a knightly gentleman, professedly a lady-servant, and the lessons that Ulrich had caught as a child from the conversation in his father's hall were reinforced by this Margrave Henry. He was taught the best style of riding, the refinements of address to ladies, and poetical composition, and assured that whoever would live worthily must be a lady's true subject. "It adorns a youth—sweet speech to women.... To succeed well with them, have sweet words with true deeds."

After four years of such instruction, his father's death called him home to inherit his property, and he spent the three years that followed by tourneying in the noviciate of knighthood. At Vienna, in 1222, during the great festival in celebration of the marriage of Leopold's daughter, where five thousand knights were present, and tourneying and other entertainments of chivalry were mingled with much dancing, Ulrich made one of the two hundred and fifty squires who received their spurs. But the occasion was otherwise memorable to him, for here he saw his lady again. She recognized him, and told one of his friends of her pleasure at seeing become a knight one who had been her page when a little fellow. The mere simple foolish thought that she would perhaps have him for her own knight, as he tells us, was sweet and good, and put him in high spirits. Indeed this was all the contentment which the blushing young knight desired:

> "Dreams are true while they last, and do we not live in dreams?"

Ulrich did not wake from his to do anything so practical as to speak face to face with her, but gaily rode off to a summer of adventure in twelve tournaments, wherein he invariably fared well, thanks to his devotion.

German sentiment has always shown a butterfly's sensibility to winter and rough weather, and with the last of autumn, Ulrich's spirit grows heavy. He longs to see his lady, he knows that now he would speak to her. There are no tourneys to distract him, and in care of heart he rose, lay down, sat, and walked. As it chanced, a cousin of his knew this only lovely one, and the taxing office of a lover's confidante fell heavily upon her, and remained for some years. After beating about the bush with her for a while, he confessed the truth, only to receive point-blank advice to give up so hopeless an aspiration. Never! on the contrary she must help him in his perseverance by visiting the lady and presenting her with a copy of the verses which Ulrich has been composing for her as a confession of his love. His cousin consented, but her mission resulted in a scornful rejection of the suit, softened by compliments upon the poem. He was advised to abandon his quest, for the lady seriously objected to his mouth. "Nothing but grim death can drive me from her; I will serve her all my life," he exclaimed. But he felt that the criticism upon his mouth was a fair one, and he determined to pay attention to it.

Poor Ulrich, with so much sentiment, yet with such physical deficiencies; with such correct perception of the use of lips, yet having such uninviting ones of his own. In one of his songs he tells us:

When a lady on her loverLooks and smiles, and for a kissShapes her lips, he can discoverNever joy so great; his blissTranscends measure:O'er all pleasures is his pleasure.

But until he was quite in his twenties, his experience of this blessedness must have been of those

"By hopeless fancy feignedOn lips that are for others";

for Ulrich confesses to the deformity of what he calls three lips; that is, a bad hare-lip.

But this protagonist of mediæval Quixotism has energy and nerve, as well as sentiment. In spite of his cousin's dissuasions (this plain-minded lady tells him to take the body God has given him, instead of arrogantly improving upon his creation), Ulrich rides off to find the best surgeon in the country, and submit to an operation. But the doctor decides that the time of year is unsuitable; he must wait until winter is past, keep his three lips until May.

At last spring comes and Ulrich returns to the doctor. Upon the way he meets a page of his lady's, to whom he confides the purpose of his journey, and whose presence he secures as a witness. Early one Monday morning the surgeon received his patient, laid out his instruments before him, and produced several straps. At sight of the latter, martial dignity recoiled, and Ulrich refused to allow himself to be bound. It was to no purpose that he was told of the danger involved in even a twitch; he said with spirit that he came of his own will, and if anything happened amiss he alone would be to blame. Whereupon he sat calmly upon a bench, and without a tremor allowed the surgeon to "cut his mouth above his teeth and farther up. He cut like a master, I endured like a man."

Ulrich describes the discomfort which he experienced during the healing of the wound, in details which give an unpleasant notion of the methods of mediæval surgery. As he was able to eat and drink scarcely anything, he wasted in flesh, and his only comfort was the thought of her for whom he had suffered. During the confinement, he composed another dancing song in her honor, which, after his recovery he entrusted to his cousin, who forwarded it with a letter of her own. Presently an answer came. The lady is to spend the next Monday night near by, in the course of a journey, and she will be very happy to see her friend's relative, and learn from himself how things are. Time changes the significance of letters, among other things. This lady-like note, which gave such a heart-leap to Ulrich's sentimental hope, interests scholars to-day as being the earliest prose letter in German.

On Tuesday morning, when Ulrich appeared at the chapel where the lady's chaplain was singing mass before her, she bowed without speaking. After the service she rode off, and Ulrich had found no chance to meet her. His cousin, however, told him that everything was favorable, and that the lady would allow him to ride with her that day. So he galloped off in gay spirits, and soon overtook the cavalcade. But alas for his self-possession; when he reaches her his head drops and he cannot find a single word. Another knight was riding with her. Ulrich's heart makes a speech to his body, reproaching it for cowardice; "If you go on without speaking to her now, she will never be good to you again." So he rides up to her and gets a sweet glance, but still he cannot speak. Heart nudges Body and whispers: "Speak now, speak now, speak now!" All through the day Body tries, he tries over and over, but he cannot. Alas, as a poet of his own day said:

"Mit gedanken wirt erworben niemer wîbes kint: . . . . Des enkan sî wizzen niht."[5]

When they reach their lodging-place for the night, he wishes to assist the only one in dismounting, but she is not sufficiently flattered by his attentions to accept them; she says that he is sick and useless, and not strong enough to help her down. The attending gentlemen laugh merrily at that, and the ever sweet, constant, good, and so forth, as she slides from her horse, catches hold of Ulrich's hair, without any one's noticing it (however that can have been done), and pulls a lock out by the roots. "Take this for being afraid," she whispers; "I have been deceived by other accounts of you." Reproaching himself, and wishing God to take his life, he stood gawkily where she left him, absorbed in remorse for his awkwardness, until a knight admonished him to step aside and allow the ladies to go by to their rooms. Whereupon he rode off to his inn, and swore that he was ill.

As he tossed restlessly through the night, he talked with himself as usual, lamenting his birth, and assuring himself that should he live a thousand years he could never again be happy. "Not to speak one word to her! My worthlessness has lost my lady." But in the morning he rode up to her on the street. No silence this time: "Thy grace, gracious lady! Graciously be gracious to me. Thou art my joy's abiding place, the festival of my joys."

Like many shy people, Ulrich talked fluently enough when he was once started, and he was only in the midst of his protestations when the lady interrupted him. "Hush, you are too young; ride on before me. Talking may hurt you, it never can help you. It would be amiss for others to hear what you are saying. Leave me in peace; you grow troublesome." Then she beckoned to another knight, and directed that she should never again be attended by less than two gentlemen.

It was in the book of lady-service that no repulse was a discouragement. "This morning," says the heroine in Bret Harte's parody of *Jane Eyre*, "this morning he flung his boot at me! Now I know he loves me." Ulrich rode off, thinking that he had met with good success in telling her a part of his love, before the interruption.

Another summer passed in tourneying, and during another winter he tried to amuse himself by making poetry for his lady. This time he sent her a more pretentious tribute, his first "Büchlein," a poem of some four hundred lines. Like most of its kind, it is formal, sentimentally prolix, and supplicatory, yet not without a certain pleasant interest. He begs her from the wealth of her loveliness to grant him some trifling favor which she never can miss:

What is worse the bloomy heath,If a few flowers for the sakeOf a garland some one break?

He wishes it were himself that the messenger is about to deliver to her:

Little book, I fain would be,When thou comest, changed to thee.When her fair white hand receivesThine assemblement of leaves,And her glances, shyly playing,Thee so happy are surveying.And her red mouth comes close by,I would steal a kiss, or die.

But the unsatisfactory manuscripts were returned at once. The lady told the bearer that she recognized the merit of the poetry, but she would have nothing to do with it. Like many poets of those days when monks and ladies constituted the educated classes, like his predecessor, the great master of high mediæval romance, Ulrich could neither read nor write, and for such delicate personal affairs as correspondence with his lady he depended upon his confidential clerk. This confidant of his passion was absent when the "Büchlein" came back, but the eager eyes of the poet looked through the pages over which they had evidently wandered before he dismissed his labors to their fate, repeating the lines from memory as he looked over the characters which should interpret his loving patience to the lady who would not let him speak it to her; and as he looked, he detected an addition to what he had sent, an appendix of ten lines. The slighted letter found a home in his bosom, and for ten days he awaited his secretary's return. His happy hopes—those ten days were so cheerful. But when the little response was at last interpreted, away with hopes and cheerfulness. To make plainness trebly plain, his cruel correspondent had copied out three times the sentiment: "Whoever desires what he should not, has refused himself."

Summer again, and the lover has diversion in the sports of chivalry. Any one interested in the details of mediæval tournaments will find in Ulrich's narrative a valuable and lively record of the tourney held at Friesach in 1224. His sense for material splendor is well shown by his full accounts of the costuming and tent equipments. The trustworthiness of the minor points may be questioned when we recall that the *Frauendienst* was composed more than thirty years later, but as a sketch of thirteenth-century chivalry, no doubt it is accurate. The heralds running hither and thither, and shouting as they arranged for the contests, with their cries to "good gallant knights to risk honor, goods, and life for true women"; the squires crowding the ways, loud noise of drums, flute-playing, blowing of horns, great trumpeting,—we have the old picture, made vivid in English by Chaucer in the *Knight's Tale*, and by Tennyson.

Ulrich rode in disguise, prompted by the sentimentalist's self-consciousness, always delighted in attracting attention and making himself talked of. According to his own account, he did good hearty tourneying, breaking ten spears with one antagonist, seven with another, five with a third, six with a fourth, in a single day. The meeting continued for ten days, and Ulrich grows prolix in his particulars, though he is modest enough about his own exploits, pronouncing himself neither the best nor the worst of the participants. The accidents of jousting, through which many were left at Friesach with broken limbs and other injuries, and the misfortunes which compelled others to have recourse to the Jews for loans, did not disturb the musical contestant. At the end he rode cheerfully off to his cousin with another song for the same inattentive ear. She promised to report, as she sent it, that no one in the great tourney had excelled him.

This lyric is the poem by which modern German students of their old literature have been best pleased, and we shall hardly dissent from Scherer's commendation. For it is both a typical minnesong, in its treatment of nature and love, and also fortunate in its union of sentiment, force, finish, and a ring of personal meaning. Omitting two of its stanzas, it goes as follows:

Now the little birds are singingIn the wood their darling lay;In the meadow flowers are springing,Confident in sunny May.So my heart's bright spirits seemFlowers her goodness doth embolden;For in her my life grows golden,As the poor man's in his dream.

Ah, her sweetness! Free from turningIs her true and constant heart;Till possession banish yearning,Let my dear hope not depart.Only this her grace I'll pray:Wake me from my tears, and afterSighs let comfort come and laughter;Let my joy not slip away.

Blissful May, the whole world's anguishFinds in thee its single weal;Yet the pain whereof I languish,Thou, nor all the world, canst heal.What least joy may ye impart,She so dear and good denied me?In her comforts ever hide me,All my life her loving heart.

But elegant and tender as in the original these verses are, their object returned a slighting answer, and added that the messenger must not be sent again. People would come to have suspicions. Ulrich made another set of verses, and went off to another joust. There one of his fingers was seriously wounded, and in his anxiety to save it he offered a surgeon a thousand pounds for a cure. The treatment was unsuccessful, and, after showing a good deal of temper, he went to a new surgeon, on the way beguiling himself of his pain by composing another poem upon the old theme. But a shock was at hand; a friend divulged to him his closely kept secret. "This lady [still unnamed to us] is the May-time of your heart." What though this friend believed that the lady cared for him? "My head sank down, my heart sighed, my mouth was dumb," in terror lest it might be through his fault that the object of his devotion had been discovered. For secrecy was the first of a chivalric lover's virtues, even about the object of his passion. Yet the pain was not without compensation, inasmuch as this gentleman, who declared that he had already kept the secret for two years and a half, volunteered to make another appeal. So off to the home of the inexorable went anew the story of unflinching devotion, the loss of a finger in a tournament for her glory not unmentioned. Ulrich's cause was pleaded with fervor, and in winning style. The lover was praised and prayed for. The song he had sent was even sung, instead of being formally delivered. A faithful and versatile legate was this proxy wooer, but it was all to no purpose. The lady declared that she would grow old in entire ignorance of any love but her husband's. She warned the messenger that Ulrich would find himself in trouble if he should persist in annoying her with such sentimental folly; she would not receive such attentions from the highest-born—not even from a king.

The news saddened, but did not cast down. "What if she refuses me?" cried Ulrich; "that shall not disturb me. If she hates me to-day, I will serve her so that later she shall like me. Were I to give up for a cold greeting, could a little word drive me away from my high hope, I should have no sound mind or manly mood. Whatever the true, sweet one does to me, for that I must be grateful." But now another summer was over, and he diverted himself by a pilgrimage to Rome. After Easter he returned, on his way composing this sweetly conceived and rather pretty lyric:

Ah, see, the touch of spring Hath graced the wood with green;And see, o'er the wide plainSweet flowers on every spray.The birds in rapture sing;Such joy was never seen:Departed all their pain,Comfort has come with May.

May comforts all that lives,Except me, love-sick man;Love-stricken is my heart,This drives all joys away.When life some pleasure gives,In tears my heart will scanMy face, and tell its smart;How then can pleasure stay?

Vowed constantly to wooHigh love am I; that goodWhile I pursue, I seeNo promise of success.Pure lady, constant, true,The crown of womanhood,Think graciously of me,Through thy high worthiness.

The knight passed his summer in Steierland under arms, and after pleasant experiences he sent his messenger again, only to have his suit repelled with the same coldness and decision as before. The report was even more discouraging, for the lady, who had been told of his losing a finger in her service, had now learned that he still had it; nor was she moved by the assurance that it was almost useless. The desire to keep the wounded member had led him to large expense of money and time, but he cared for it no longer. He set about the composition of another long elegy, which explains how his heart loves her, and weeps for her favor, as a poor and orphaned child weeps after comfort; so ardently he loves her, that he gladly sacrifices anything, and as a pledge of his constant fidelity, he sends her one of his fingers, lost in that service for which it was born.

After the poem was ready, he directed a goldsmith to make a fine case, in which he enclosed it. But he put in something more; he had the convalescent finger amputated, and sent it to the chiding critic as a proof that he had not lied in saying that he had lost it for her. Yet even this failed to please so unsympathetic a mistress. She said she wondered how any one could be so foolish as to cut off his finger: he would have been able to serve ladies better by keeping it. However, she would retain the token of his consideration, but a thousand years of his service would be lost on her. Ulrich was jubilant, for he was confident that with this memento, she would always think of him.[6]

Now a large idea visits this sanguine gentleman. Gone to Rome on a pilgrimage, that is what he will pretend; he rigs himself out with a wallet and staff which he obtains from a priest, and trudges off. But something more novel and magnificent is haunting his ingenious mind. It is to Venice that he goes—cautiously, so as not to be observed. Upon his arrival, he takes lodgings in an out-of-the-way inn, so that no one may hear of him. There he spends the winter, making a liberal expenditure for costumes for himself and a retinue. He dresses himself as Queen Venus, in complete feminine attire, even to the long braids of hair which figure so prominently in the descriptions of the ladies of that age.

When spring came, he sent a courier over the route that he intended to take on his journey homeward, with a circular-letter that contained a list of thirty places at which Lady Venus would appear, and joust with all contestants. A ring which makes beautiful and keeps true love, was offered to whoever might break a spear against her. If she should cast a knight down, he should become a loyal knight to women everywhere; if he were to overthrow her, she would give him her horse. But to no one would she show her face or hand.

Thirty days later he started on his disguised errantry. His retinue consisted of a marshal, a cook, a banner-bearer, two trumpeters, three boys to take charge of three sumpters, three squires for the three war-steeds, four finely dressed squires, each holding three spears, two maids—good-looking, he tells us,—and two fiddlers.

Who raised my spirits, fiddling loudA marching tune, which made me proud.

Behind these he rode himself, dressed, like the entire cavalcade, entirely in white,—cape, hood, shirt, coat reaching to his feet, embroidered silk gloves, and those hair-braids hanging to his waist. "In my love-longing heart, I rejoiced thus to serve my lady."

The narrative of this "Venus-journey" is prolonged, detailed, and tedious, and only two or three episodes need be mentioned. At Treviso, a crowd of women are gathered about his lodging, when he comes out on his way to early mass, and he takes comfort in thinking how well-dressed he is. In the church, a countess suggests kissing him, conformably to the kiss of peace custom; the attraction is stronger than the desire for disguise, and he lifts his veil. She sees that Lady Venus is a man, but she kisses him nevertheless. "That raised my spirits," Ulrich confides to us, "for a lady's kiss is delightful"; and he goes on to say that "every one who ever kissed a lady's mouth knows that nothing is so sweet as the kiss of a noble lady. A high-born true woman who has a red mouth and a fair body, whenever she kisses a man he can judge of a lady's kiss, and of it he is ever glad. A lady's kiss is still better than good, and it fills a heart with joy." No wonder that many ladies collected at his inn, to bid so sentimental a knight God-speed. From their prayers he assures us that he gained good fortune, "for God cannot slight ladies' petitions," an imputation of gallantry to God, for which we find curious mediæval parallels.

Wherever the knight goes, numerous contestants are awaiting him, in this idle age when no one had anything to do. Some of these, also, assume disguises, one as a monk, another in female costume, his shield and spear æsthetic with flowers. But the travelling combatant is always the winner. At one point during the journey he steals off for a couple of days to a place which he has never mentioned previously: namely, to his home. The love-stricken lady-servant speaks with the most unaffected simplicity of the joy with which he rode away to see his wife:

> "Who was just as dear to me as she could be.... The good woman received me just as a lady should receive her very dear husband. I had made her happy by my visit. My arrival had taken away her sadness. She was glad to see me, and I was glad to see her; with kisses the good woman received me. The true woman was glad to see me, and joyously I took my ease and pleasure there two days."

This appears tautological, but it also seems sincere.

But a wound was in store for his sensibility. One day he had gone to a retired place for a bath, and his attendant had gone to bring a suit. While thus left quite alone and unprotected, a lady sent by her servant a suit of female garments, a piece of tapestry, a coat, a girdle, a fine buckle, a garland, a ring with a ruby red as a lady's sweet mouth, and a letter. To receive such a gift from a lady not one's love was treason. He bade the page take the things away, but he would not; nay, he presently returned with two others, carrying fresh beautiful roses, which they strewed all about Ulrich in the bath, while he raged and fumed to think of the insult offered to his unprotected condition. To think of receiving a gift from any but his own lady! And, of all gifts, a ring!

The next present that came was received very differently. After all these years of neglect, the mistress of his life sent Ulrich an affectionate message, and a ring which her white hand had worn for ten years, as a token that she took part in the honors which he was gaining, and rejoiced in his worthiness. Possibly the knight's name was gaining currency as genuinely valorous. But fancy his ecstasy! "This little ring shall ever lift up my heart. Well for me that I was born, and that I found a lady so true, sweet, blissful, lady of all my joys, brightness of my heart's joys," and so forth. He was informed that many knights were waiting to contest with him at Vienna.

"What harm can happen to me, since my lady is gracious? If for every knight there were three, I could master them all."

Outside of amorous and knightly themes, Ulrich's mind is not active, but he occasionally shows a philosophical observation on social topics, as in the present context, where he comments on female vanity in dress:

> "Woman's nature, young and old, likes many clothes. Even if she does not wear them all, she is pleased to have them, so that she can say, 'an if I liked, I could be better dressed than other people.' Good clothes are becoming to beautiful women, and my foolish masculine opinion is that a man should take pleasure in dressing them well, since he should hold his wife as his own body."

Certainly Ulrich took pleasure in dressing himself well.

The Venus-journey ended, and Ulrich counted up the results. Two hundred and seventy-one of his spears had been broken, and he had broken three hundred and seven; he had brought honor upon his lady by his loyalty and valor; and had shown her constant devotion, even though he had momentarily fallen in love with a bewitching woman at one of his stopping-places, and taken advantage of his disguise to kiss various fair ones at mass. Is it possible that the anonymous heroine heard of such trivial infidelities? At any rate, the next visit of the messenger brought a bitter dismissal, with cruel charges of inconstancy. She would always hate him, and never hold him dear; she was angry with herself for giving him a ring; she bade him return it at once. Alas, poor Ulrich! Never had he entertained a false thought; if he had ever been guilty of one, he would in no wise have survived it. "I sat weeping like a child; from weeping I was almost blind. I wrung my hands pitilessly; in my distress my limbs cracked as one snaps dry wood." Well may the poet declare that exhibition of grief no child's play. As the lover and his bosom friend sat weeping together, Ulrich's brother-in-law admonished him that such behavior disgraced the name of knight; moreover, there was no reason for melancholy now, when the champion ought to be happy in the fine reputation just made. "If women hear how you are behaving, they will always hate you for this weak mood." Ulrich tried to tell about his grief for the lady whom he had served so long, but the strain was too great: "The blood in truth burst out from my mouth and my nose, so that I was all blood." It was perhaps natural for his friend to thank God that "before his death he had been permitted to see one man who truly loves." Yet he bade him be courageous. "Nothing helps so much with ladies as good courage. Melancholy doesn't succeed with them at all. Joyousness always has served well with women."

Water is stable compared with Ulrich's temperament. Close upon the anguish of this renewed rejection he goes home for a ten-days' visit with his wife,—"my dear wife, who could not be dearer to me even though I had another woman for the lady of my life." Within eight lines this mercurial poet speaks of his comfort with his wife, and of the suffering of his love-languishing heart.

Another message from his dream brought a renewed expression of coldness. She felt kindly to him, but she never would grant favor to any one. But another song and messenger secure at last the promise of an interview. Yet notice the conditions. Evidently this lady was a humorist, to whom her former page was amusing when her less complaisant mood did not find him tiresome. And perhaps she thought that he could not accept her terms. She says she will see him if he will come the next Sunday morning before breakfast, dressed in poor clothes, and in company with a squad of lepers who have a camp near her castle. But even then he is to indulge in no hope of her love. The distance is so great that he thinks he will be unable to cover it in time; but he is told that he must, for "women are very strange; they wish men constantly to carry out their desires, and to any one who fails to do so they are not well disposed." On Saturday he rode thirty-six miles, lost two horses by the forced journey, very likely over rough country, and was wearied by the exertion of so hard an effort. But he succeeded, and as soon as they reach the neighborhood of the castle, he and his two companions put on poor clothes—the shabbiest they could procure,—and with leper cups and long knives for their safety among such outcasts of society, they go to the spot where thirty lepers are huddled together. Mediæval charity and religion are illustrated by this incident; the miserable beggars explain that a lady of the castle is ill, and therefore they often receive food and money in recompense for their prayers for her recovery. Beating his clapper like one of them, he goes toward the castle gate, and meets an envoy maid who bids him beware of failing to obey every command literally, and adds that her mistress will not see him yet awhile. That personal vanity which always marked him had submitted to stains of herbs to disguise his face, as well as to miserable and ragged dress, and off he went, in the servitude of love, and sat among the lepers, ate and drank among them—nay, even went about begging for scraps, which, however, he threw under a bush. The foul odors and the filthiness of the wretches about him made the day almost insufferable, but at last night came, and he hid himself in a field of grain, getting well stung by insects and drenched in a cold storm. But he told himself that "whoever has in his troubles sweet anticipation, he can endure them." In the morning he went to the castle again, and was encouraged to believe that he would be received that evening. So he returned and ate with the beggars; then he escaped to a wood, and with true old German nature-sentiment, he sat down where the sun fell through the trees and listened to the birds—many were singing—and forgot the cold.

Toward evening he secured another interview with the maid, and received directions for the night. He and his companion hid in the ditch before the castle, skulking from the observation of the patrol, until well after dark; then when the signal light appeared at a certain window he went beneath it, and found a rope made of clothes hanging down. In this he fastened himself, and hands above began to raise him, but when he was half way up they could raise him no farther, and he was let down to the ground. This happened three times; and yet, guileless Ulrich, you had no glimmering that perhaps it was a joke? The companion was lighter than his lord, and it occurred to the two that they had better change places. So they did, and the substitute was lifted into the window by the waiting ladies above, and then Ulrich himself arrived there. He was given a coat (an accident below had compelled him to leave his on the ground), and, blissful moment, he was ushered into the presence of the woman whom he had so long served without even a glimpse. It was a brilliant social scene which broke upon those enamoured eyes, indeed too brilliant and too social to correspond with a lover's sentiment for "dual solitude." His soul's desire, richly dressed, sat upon a couch, surrounded by a bevy of ladies. Her husband, it is true, was not present, but with an absence of tact (as it must have seemed to Ulrich) she fell to talking about him and her complete happiness in his love. Their mutual confidence is so strong that he is quite willing to have her receive any visitors whom she pleases, and she added that her true mind served him better than any safeguard which he could put upon her. Awkward as such a line of conversation made it, Ulrich began to tell the story of his heart, and entreats her to respond to his devotion. She assured him that she had no thought of ever loving him; she had consented to this interview only to assure him of her kindly feeling, and satisfy him from her own lips that he must cherish no romantic hope. If he continued to ask her to love him, he should lose her favor. "I was horrified," he declares, "and started up at the threat."

At this point in the interview he withdraws to talk to his cousin, who was with other ladies in an adjoining apartment, and who advised him to return and plead again. But an abrupt dismissal sends him into a moody reflection, which culminates in a desperate resolve. Now or never; he sends her word of his determination, and then rushes in and tells her that if she will not say she loves him, he will kill himself then and there. The lady sees that such a suicide would be compromising, and tries to persuade him that perhaps she may some time. Ah, no such coyness; she must confess her love to-night. Finally, as a last resource, she thinks of employing the usual right of a courted woman—putting her lover to a test of his devotion. He has already given her so many that a trifling, a merely formal one will serve now. Let him just get into the clothes-rope again and be lowered part way down, and pulled back; then she will say she loves him. A glimmer of suspicion flits over his mind, but she gives him her hand as a pledge, and he gets into the rope. Now he is hanging outside the window, still holding the dear hand, and such sweet things as she whispers, as she leans out—no knight was ever so dear to her; now comes his contentment, all his troubles are past now! She even coddles his chin with her disengaged hand, and bids him kiss her. Kiss her! In his joy he lets go the hand he was holding, to throw both arms about her neck, when suddenly he is dropped to the ground so swiftly "that he ran great peril of his life."[7]

In the rooms above a score of voices ringing with laughter, on the ground a too credulous child of Mars and Venus, cursing his day. Ulrich spies a deep pool and is about to drown himself, when his companion arrives with a little present sent by the lady. She promises—(the gentleman afterward confesses that this is a falsehood of his own to preserve Ulrich from despair)—that if he will return in three weeks, she will assure him of her real affection. But now it is near day, and they must hasten off; providentially there is a tournament awaiting them, which will distract his attention. But he sends his friend back to have a talk with the lady, who is in a rather humorous mood, and says that Ulrich made so much noise when he fell that one of the guard thought it was the Devil. But though she laughs, she evidently has had enough of such fun, for she tells the messenger that if his lord wishes her favor he must make the journey oversea. Ulrich agrees to go, but he is warned against the almost hopeless dangers of that most formidable of pilgrimages; he is reminded that no one ever took such a perilous journey except for God, and that he would surely sacrifice his soul, if he lost his life thus for a woman.

But one grows tired of the story, which runs on with ups and downs, over the long thirteen years through which Ulrich served this lady. Toward the end of the period he was plainly growing impatient. He wrote more lyrics, which suggest here and there that devotion without love in return is foolish, and that he is contemplating a change. Finally he conceived himself treated shamefully (we are not told what the discourtesy was which he could not idealize), and he made a final break with his old worship. But now the time passed wearily, and he felt that he must still have a lady to serve. "How joyfully once the days went by; alas, no longer have I any service to render. How happy ladies' service makes one." But the knight has learned the lesson of his trials, and this time he arranges for a judicious passion. He runs over all his female acquaintance, to see which of them he had best select. Finally he fixes upon one who, of course, is beautiful and good, and wholly free from change; who has finished manners and gentle ways, chastity and force of character, and to her he offers his service, which she accepts.

From this point in Ulrich's memoirs we have an increasing number of lyrics; he likes them all, but complains that one or two were not appreciated by the public, though whoever was clever enough to understand his poetry, he tells us, did appreciate it. Perhaps we are not clever enough to understand it all; but some of the songs, as he himself says, "are good for dancing and very cheerful; the martial ones were gladly sung when in the jousts fire sprung from helmets," and more than one of his poems is a contribution to the graceful though minor work of the later minnesingers. For example:

Summer-hued,Is the wood,Heath and field; debonairNow is seenWhite, brown, green,Blue, red, yellow, everywhere.EverythingYou see springJoyously, in full delight;He whose painsDear love deignsWith her favor to requite—Ah, happy wight.

Whosoe'erKnows love's care,Free from care well may be;Year by yearBrightness clearOf the May shall he see.Blithe and gayAll the playOf glad love shall he fulfil;Joyous livingIs in the givingOf high love to whom she will,Rich in joys still.

He's a churlWhom a girlLovingly shall embrace,Who'll not cry"Blest am I"—Let none such show his face.This will cure you(I assure you)Of all sorrows, all alarms;What alloyIn his joyOn whom white and pretty armsBestow their charms?

And again:

Sweet, in whom all things behooving,Virtue, brightness, beauty, meet,Little troubles thee this loving,Thou art safe above it, sweet.My love-trials couldst thou feelFrom thy dainty lips should stealSighs like mine, as deep and real.

Sir, what is love? Prithee, answer;Is it maid or is it man?And explain, too, if you can, sir,How it looks; though I beganLong ago, I ask in vain;Everything you know explain,That I may avoid its pain.

Sweet, love is so strong and mightyThat all countries own her sway;Who can speak her power rightly?Yet I'll tell thee what I may.She is good and she is bad;Makes us happy, makes us sad;Such moods love always had.

Sir, can love from care beguile usAnd our sorrowing distress?With fair living reconcile us,Gaiety and worthiness?If her power hath controlledEverything as I've just told,Sure her grace is manifold.

Sweet, of love there's more to tell thee;Service she with rapture pays;With her joys and honors dwell; weLearn from her dear virtue's ways.Mirth of heart and bliss of eyeWhom she loves shall satisfy;Nor will she higher good deny.

Sir, I fain would win her wages,Her approval I would seek;Yet distress my mind presages;Ah, for that I am too weak.Pain I never can sustain.How may I her favors gain?Sir, the way you must explain.

Sweet, I love thee; be not cruel;Thou to love again must try.Make a unit of our dual,That we both become an "I."Be thou mine and I'll be thine."Sir, not so; the hope resign.Be your own, and I'll be mine."

The latter part of this prolix autobiography is occupied by a detailed account of a long tourneying trip, which he contrived as a parallel to his Venus-journey, this time under the disguise of King Arthur. But the narration of that ends at last, and Ulrich becomes reflective upon the seasons and his lady. "Whoever sorrows at winter, and is made glad by summer, lives like the bird which rejoices in sunny May. How distressing is bad weather! Yet whatever the weather, her goodness gives me joy which storms cannot disturb." Presently he tells us his feelings about the life around him, for the social critics of mediævalism felt the inequalities of fortune and happiness quite as strongly as do the social critics of to-day. Some time earlier Ulrich, in criticising a number of knights whom he met, showed a noteworthily refined feeling for generous qualities, and resistance against hardness and selfish aims. In spite of this love-singer's belief in cheerfulness ("no one does well to be sad except about sins," he wrote), the roughness of the age troubled him, as it had troubled earlier and greater authors of his nation. "Instead of being good, the rich work one another harm; the only profession is that of plundering, the service of ladies is forsaken. The young men are spendthrifts, and with pillaging consume their youth." Indeed, the golden hour of chivalry had struck when Ulrich wrote, in his later life, just past the middle of the thirteenth century. But this sentimental absurdity, whose fanciful devotion and melodramatic moonings we find so preposterous, kept a strain of the higher manhood. He was good-hearted; he believed in the refined side of life, so far as he knew it; in a rough time and place he loved gentleness; though born with a large streak of the fool, he had also a pleasant element of the simple-minded gentleman; and as he grew old amid fading ideals, over which he had hung with effeminately romantic faith, the brutal and joyless hardness of men perplexed and saddened him. Yet his simplicity was his trouble's best physician; nature, the beauty and goodness of true womanhood, his sense of inner virtue as opposed to worldly estimates, and his poetry—in these he found comfort.

"Whatever people have done, I have been happy and sung of my love."

After Ulrich has told the story of his worldly and sentimental career, he stops to think over the cause to which that career has been consecrated. Has he made a mistake? Never! "When beauty and goodness unite in woman, she is admirable; one whose goodness is clothed with a noble spirit wears the best of garments. Even though a woman has little beauty, if she has the raiment of goodness, men yet call her fair. Be sure that no clothes better become a lady than goodness—it is better than beauty, though that is excellent. By goodness a poor woman will become truly a lady, and this the rich cannot be without it; nay, shapely and noble though she may be, without this she is still no womanly woman." ...

"Whoever loves the sight of pretty women," he goes on, "and will not notice their goodness but only their bright charm, is like one who gathers pretty flowers for their bright beauty's sake, and twines them into a garland; then, finding that they are not fragrant, he is sorry that he gathered them. But whoever understands plants, lets those grow which have no sweet odor, and breaks off fragrant flowers."

For over thirty years he has served ladies, and he knows no truth so certain as this, that nothing equals the mutual happiness of a true woman and a loving man.

Yet sentiment can play only a minor part in life, after all. There are four main objects of exertion, and upon these, as he ends his book, the poet stops to reflect: The grace of God, honor, ease, and wealth. Some strive for one, some for another, while others aim ineffectively at all, win none, and hate themselves.

And what has this old German gallant to say of himself? In all these revelations of his life, we catch no suggestions of selfishness or meanness, but while fancying himself enacting high chivalric drama, he has been wearing cap, and bells, and motley, lance in his left hand, a bauble in his right. Then, too, he has been so self-satisfied with his rôle. Well, the play is finished now, and Ulrich is sitting in the green-room, thinking. His coat is flung aside, with one last jingle the bells fall to the floor, he has dropped his bauble, and as he bows his head and in his musing runs his fingers through his hair, the coxcomb falls too. It is here in the green-room that he speaks his epilogue:

"Of this last class am I; I have lived my life trying not to give up the three for any one. I desired and even hoped that I might obtain all the four. This hope has still deceived me, and I am made a fool by it. One day I will serve Him who has given me soul, life, thought, whatever I have; the next as a man I will strive for honor; then for wealth; on the fourth day I am for ease. Thus inconstant, I have passed my entire life."

Nothing accomplished—nothing even steadily aimed at. Nothing? With characteristic buoyancy the gray-haired poet puts aside this sombre mood of dissatisfaction with his fifty odd years. For in one point, at least, he has been true. In this book, written only because his lady commanded, he has spoken very many sweet words for worthy women, and throughout his life he has been faithful to his love. "And I do believe that the very true sweet God, through his very high goodness, will think on my fidelity to her, and my constant service."

NEIDHART VON REUENTHAL, AND HIS BAVARIAN PEASANTS.

Our liveliest pictures of old German peasantry come, as we should expect, from a singer of the knightly class. The masses had fewer and of course less accomplished poets, and these would be most likely to please their audiences by touching with the glamour of fashionable life such work as they cared to make contemporary and imitative. Realistic social transcripts usually come from culture. It may be that Neidhart von Reuenthal had been brought up at the ducal court or in a castle, but there is as good reason for conjecturing that his origin was among the scenes of country life that he describes. Most of the courtly poets belonged to the lower class of knights, and between this and the better order of peasants there was no wide dividing line; indeed, a farmer with a little land of his own and four free ancestors ("von allen vieren anen ein gebûre," as Neidhart says bitterly of his enemy the swaggering Ber), by the old Saxon law stood higher than a knight not of free blood. The agricultural class in the thirteenth century was becoming more impatient of the costly conflicts of their military superiors and was also suffering severely from the pillaging domestic raids of lawless knights, who, as they grew bolder, established centres of reckless freebooting to which they attracted wayward youth of the middle classes. Cities were also getting larger, and the tradesmen joined with the established gentry in thinking slightingly of the farming population. Accordingly there was jealousy on one side and arrogance on the other, yet there was still a meeting-place between the two classes. Depleted nobles would marry daughters of wealthy peasants, and a gentleman whose fief lay among well-to-do farmers might easily meet them in social relations.

A grant from the Bavarian Duke evidently isolated Neidhart from his own companions, and he appears to have mingled freely with the peasantry, though we cannot determine how early the contact began. He was born in the latter part of the twelfth century, we may say about 1185, perhaps, and with the exception of absence on Leopold VII's crusade of 1217-1219, he apparently kept his home in his native Bavaria until about 1230, when he lost the Duke's favor and turned as a homeless wanderer to Austria, where he received welcome and another fief. The last date inferred from his songs is 1236, in connection with the Emperor's coming, and he was dead before the composition of Meier Helmbrecht, which is earlier than 1250.

So far as imitations prove popularity, he was one of the most popular of mediæval poets. It is easy to understand the pleasure that his verses must have given, striking as they did into a new field, and executed with literary skill, full of verve and humor, and appealing to strong class prejudice. We must think of him as a gentleman fond of society, of refined courtly habits, with an aristocratic contempt for pinchbeck upstarts, yet not unwilling now and then to play the good-natured acquaintance with middle-class people.

Though he ranks as a knight, his tastes were not military. He was lively, quick-witted, and satirical; clever at musical invention; genuinely interested in poetry. Moreover, he gave early evidence of an independent literary taste, that dared to yawn at the methods practised by the great minnesingers of his youth. By his singing he had obtained sufficient favor with the Duke to receive a fief though away among the peasantry; yet rather than relinquish a home of his own, that constant dream of his profession, he made the merriest and the best of the time he needed to spend on his estate.

The feeling for spring is largely an animal sensation, as the lambs in the pasture, or dogs on the green, or little children remind us. The comparison of loving something "as goats love the spring," goes back to Greek literature. It has also been habitually associated with physical sentiment, as the splendid proëmium of Lucretius suggests. With this buoyancy of spirits and emotional susceptibility, serious minds touched with poetry have associated various deep and beautiful moods. But the moral element that enters into such spring poems as Wordsworth's, is not present in mediæval literature. There we find poets feeling spring as animals, as children, as lovers. Those were out-of-door generations; hunting, riding, fighting, and enjoying themselves beneath the open sky, were their chief employments. They found winter travel hard, for they had no beaten roads; it caused a dreary interruption to their principal engagements, and to a large extent confined them in narrow quarters, not too comfortably warmed. In spite of all the amusements that could be provided, the time must have dragged. If Romans could cry out as Ovid did at the significance of spring, what must the season have meant to the castled sons of central Europe. It is not strange then that their nature-worship instituted in early times a festival to the genial conqueror of frost and snow, and that this ceremony, as the old superstitions died away, was continued in graceful traditions of village customs. The first flowers or the earliest boughs in leaf served as the signal for the ceremonial welcome of April or May. With widely varying details, the youth of the parish would stream out to the fields or woods, and come back singing spring catches, and dancing that long, skipping forward step which they practised out-of-doors, carrying with them trophies of the season. Sometimes they fastened the first violet to a pole, and setting it up danced around it; sometimes they danced about the first linden that appeared in leaf. It is the linden that the poets are continually mentioning, whether in the centre of the courtyard or in the field, and the tree suggests the social life of the old times as happily as the pine under which Charlemagne sat, in the great chanson, suggests the imperial master.

Customs related in Herrick's *Going a-Maying,* such as the decoration of the houses of favorites with early greenery and the processions of girls and young men to the woods and fields, were familiar in Germany long before. Exercises to welcome spring became not only a social but even—so far as the rude country songs went—a literary habit. The earlier ritual dance around some altar or symbol of the summer deity grew into an entertainment from which all sense of its original significance had passed away. These celebrations became the main social feature of the warm months. At one time partners appear to have been taken for the year (a passage in *Wilhelm Meister* reminds us of this usage), but not in the period before us. A summons to a holiday dance (and the large number of church festivals made holidays frequent) was usually given by a musician playing or singing through the street. The young men and women, and not infrequently their elders, came to the customary field, dressed for the gaiety; as they went along, tossing and catching bright-colored balls. This favorite ball-playing, mentioned by more than one poet of the age as a sign of spring, and especially entered into by girls, often formed a prelude to the dance. For one thing it gave the girls a way of choosing their partners, for the man who caught the ball tossed by a girl, according to some usages, could claim the right to dance with her. An anonymous poet of the thirteenth century gives a lively picture of one of these scenes.

> "All the time the young people are passing ball on the street. This is the earliest sport of summer, and as they play they scream. What if the rustic lad gives me a shove? How rude he is as he darts here and there, flying and chasing and playing tricks with the ball. Then two by two they have a hoppaldy dance about the fiddle, as if they wanted to fly."

As one of the fellows holds the ball,

> "What pretty speeches the girls make him, how they shriek, how wild they get. While he's hesitating to whom he'll throw, they stretch out their hands; now you're my friend (geveterlin),—throw it down here to me ... Jiutelin and Elsemuot hurry after it. Whoever gets it is the best one. Krumpolt ran, and cried, 'Throw it to me, and I'll throw it back.' In the scrimmage some of the girls get pushed down, and an accident happens to Eppe, the prettiest one in the field. But she picks herself up, and tosses the ball into the air. All scream, 'Catch it! catch it!'

No girl can play better than she does; she judges the ball so well, and is such a sure catch."

Another way of choosing partners was by presenting garlands, and one of the prettiest of the spring customs was the walk to the fields and woods after flowers for wreaths, either to give away or to wear. So one of the Latin songs describes young people going out,—

"Juvenes ut flores accipiantEt se per odores reficiantVirgines assumant alacriter,Et eant in prata floribus ornata, communiter."

It certainly is a genial phase of those old times, this out-of-door companionship of lads and lassies, gathering flowers and "dancing in the chequered shade." The custom has in a manner survived to our own day; in England, for example, Mr. Thomas Hardy has introduced such scenes very pleasantly in some of his novels, but the zest and universality of it have not descended. Even in Elizabeth's England the hobby-horse was forgot; and back in the thirteenth century the May-time amusements were being frowned away. For preachers and moralists saw much evil in these summer gaieties. It is the old story: Nature is such a puritanical stage-manager that she likes to bring on a tragedy for the after-piece to her pleasant comedy, and she is best satisfied when we take warning from the practice and stay away from the play.

The insane frenzies into which meadow dancing was carried on some occasions, especially at the riotous midsummer festival, do not belong to our subject. Neidhart assumes a flippant tone about matters of conduct, but his treatment of the summer merrymakings is usually innocent and agreeable. He comes as an artist, to the rude material provided in the traditional village songs for these occasions, and transfers to the polished verse of Germany's already highly trained lyrical school, that fresh and gay subject-matter that is so remote from the formal phrases of most of his courtly predecessors. His songs are lyric in their introduction, but almost invariably epic or dramatic in the later stanzas, scarcely ever overstepping closely drawn lines. Whereas, Walther von der Vogelweide's work in the popular poetry retains the lyrical mood throughout, and is far less realistic, never, I believe, treating a peasant element as such. Those lyrical preludes attest Neidhart's deep sentiment for nature; we feel that, in spite of the conventionality in them. He has the rare merit of an occasional specific note, and he touches even the hackneyed expressions about birds and flowers with a contagious buoyancy. Look at a few of these introductions:

"Hedges green as gold; the heath dressed in bright roses. Come on, you fine girls: May is in the land. The linden is well hung with rich attire; now hearken, how the nightingale draws near."

"The time is here: for many a year I have not seen a fairer. The cold winter is over, and many hearts rejoice that felt its chill. The woods are in leaf. Come then with me to the linden, dear."

"Summer, a thousand welcomes! Whatever heart was wounded by the long winter is healed, its pain all gone. Thou comest welcome to the world in all lands. Through thee, rich and poor lose their sorrows, when winter has to go."

And another, which loses its effect if we neglect the long, swinging metre:

The forest for new foliage its grey dress has forsaken;And therefore now full many hearts to pleasure must awaken.The birds to whom the winter brought dismay,Have never sung so well as now the praises of the May.

The winter from the lovely heath at last has turned aside,And there the blossoms stand, arrayed in colors gaily pied.Above them May's sweet dews are lightly shed;Ah, how I wish I had a wreath, dear friend, a lady said.

This stanza moves more quickly:

Forth from your houses, children fair!Out to the street! No wind is there,Sharp wind, cold snow.The birds were dreary,They're singing cheerily;Forth to the woodland go.

After such opening stanzas comes the action of the song, almost always an expression of a girl's longing to go to the dance, and her mother's unwillingness. The burden of the remonstrances is that of the song in *Much Ado*, "Men were deceivers ever"; and though some of the conversations are amiable, often the two come to high words, and even to blows. The girl cannot think of going without her best costume, and this, in the prudent old domestic management, was always carefully folded up, and kept under lock and key. "Who gave you the right to lock up my gown?" a daughter demands. "You did not spin a thread of it. Where's the key? now open the room for me." Finally, she obtained it by stealth. "She took from the chest the gown that was laid in many small folds. To the knight of Reuenthal she threw her colored ball." But Neidhart grimly brings in her mother at the close.

Another cries: "Bring me my fine gown. The gentleman from Reuenthal has sung us a new song. I hear him singing there to the children. I must dance with him at the linden." Her mother warns her of what happened to her playmate Jiute last year, "just as her mother said." But the gentleman had sent her a lovely garland of roses, and had brought her a pair of red stockings from over the Rhine, which she was wearing then; and she had promised to let him teach her the dance. Another song represents two girls talking of the same knight from Reuenthal: "All know him, and his songs are heard everywhere. He loves me, and to please him I will lace myself trimly, and go."

Some of the mothers do more than remonstrate: "The wood is well in leaf, but my mother will not let me go. She has tied my feet with a rope. But all the same, I must go with the children to the linden in the field." Her mother overheard and threatened to punish her. "You little grasshopper, whither wilt thou hop away from the nest? Sit and sew in the sleeve for me." The girl is impudent, and the poem ends with a lively contest.

Love is too strong. "He kissed me," one of them says, "and he had some root in his mouth, so that I lost all my senses." Perhaps the high-born poet bewitched these peasant-girls; he often assures us of it. One of them is plighted to a farmer, and whenever he expects to find her at home to entertain him, she joins the dancers, as toward evening "they bend their way down the street," and throws her ball to the knightly singer. Even the mothers themselves are sometimes caught by the desire to dance with him, or at least with some of the men at the linden, and in two or three of Neidhart's sprightliest songs the tables are turned, and the daughter tries to keep her mother from the gaieties that her years have outgrown. I have translated two of these summer dance songs in their exact rhythms, and so literally as to make them appear almost bald. In the first the nature opening may be omitted.

"Mother, do not deny me,—Forth to the field I'll hie me,And dance the merry spring;'Tis ages since I heard the crowdAny new carols sing."

"Nay, daughter, nay, mine own,Thee I have all aloneUpon my bosom carried;Now yield thee to thy mother's will,And seek not to be married."

"If I could only show him!Why, mother dear, you know him,And to him I will haste;Ah, 'tis the knight of Reuenthal,And he shall be embraced.

"Such green the branches bending!The leafy weight seems rendingThe trees so thickly clad:Now be assured, dear mother mine,I'll take the worthy lad.

"Dear mother, with such burningAfter my love he's yearning,Ungrateful can I be?He says that I'm the prettiestFrom France to Germany."

Bare we saw the fields, but that is over;Now the flowers are crowding thro' the clover;At length the season that we love is here:As last year,All the heath is caught and held by roses;To roses summer brings good cheer.

Thrushes, nightingales, we hear them singing;With their loud music mount and dale are ringing:For the dear summer is their jubilee:To you and me,It brings bright sights and pleasures without number;The heath is a fair thing to see.

"Dewy grow the meadows," cried a maiden,"Branches lately bare are greenly laden:Listen! how the birds are crowning May:Come and play,For, Wierat, the leaves are on the linden;Winter, I ween, has gone away.

"This year, too, we'll dance till twilight closes;Near the wood is a great mass of roses,I'll have a garland of them, trimly made;Come, you jade,Hand in hand with a fine knight you'll see meDance in the linden shade."

"Little daughter, heed not his advances;If thou press among the knights at dances,Something not befitting such as weThere will beTrouble coming to thee, little daughter—And the young farmer thinks of thee."

"Nay, I trust to rule a knight in armor;How then should I listen to a farmer?What! you think I'd be a peasant's bride!"She replied:"He could never woo me to my liking,He'll never marry me," she cried.

At first Neidhart seems to have maintained friendly relations with the young men of the district, for we find him addressing in amicable terms even Engelmar, who later became his worst enemy, complimenting him upon his room, in a song apparently designed for a dance at his house. But it is difficult to believe that his critical genius would have gone long without expression, and he presently began amusing himself, and courting the admirations of others, by original snatches of songs that were imitated from the *trutzstrophen* of humorous, rustic, and often roughly personal verses, that were evidently in vogue among the country people before Neidhart's day. Such jeering, gibing bits of peasant fun-making would grow out of the custom of songs at these rural gatherings, like the parallel practice sometimes found with us of country valentine-parties, where personalities are touched off with the freedom of anonymous and privileged license. We can readily imagine him beginning with hits at one and another, that contained no deeper offence than an inevitable tone of his amused sense of the ridiculous. But the country gallants, already jealous of their elegant rival, whose gentlemanly prestige and courtly accomplishments would naturally make him attractive to their sweethearts, would be quick to take umbrage, and boorishly ready to manifest their displeasure. Neidhart certainly enjoyed at least as much of the poetic dower as "the hate of hate, the scorn of scorn," and must have answered their sullenness and rudeness with the contempt that falls with such a sting from gentility. Then stung himself by their bad manners, he naturally composed sharper and more direct stanzas, holding those who had offended him up to the laughter of other men, and of the tittering damsels. It does not seem probable that the most cutting and individualized of these attacks were written to be sung at dances where the victims of the satire were present. When we consider the violence and recklessness that historically marked this whole class in the thirteenth century, we are sure that the poet would hardly have survived some of the recitations. Many of them he probably composed to gratify his possibly irritated mood; for, as we shall presently see, his displeasure was deeper than the vexation of wounded social pride. But they strayed easily to the objects of their ridicule. As he strolled along the street, carrying his fiddle, and stopping to amuse himself at one house or another with any of the pretty girls whom he found idle like himself, he may have played and sung the piece over which he had just been working, or the minor singers who must have haunted him as he grew better known, would catch up and repeat far and wide the witty verses. The piece at which he was working, I said, for in an important sense the poems were professional labor. The natural comparison of the minnesinger on his farm to Ovid among the Goths, loses most of its force when we reflect that Neidhart's absences from his various little Romes were in some sense at his own pleasure, and that he must have kept riding about from castle to castle, and have made frequent sojourns at his patron's court, in the exercise of his now established musical vocation. The better his songs, the surer his hold on the Duke's favor, and as his prestige might rise throughout the country, the more cordial his greeting would be, and the more generous his dismission whenever he chose to go. These mediæval poets were more than careless rhymsters: painstaking labor was assumed as necessary for success. Their poetry was as subtle and difficult as the schoolmen's philosophy; though we may not care much for either, we at least respect the skill with which they mastered self-enforced technical difficulties. Arnaut Daniel's contest for a wager with another troubadour (King Richard was to decide which produced the cleverer poem), illustrates the statement that time was thought necessary for composition. The Provençal biography tells us that the contestants were shut up in separate rooms, and only ten days were allowed each for preparing his song. In Neidhart's seclusion on his fief, then, he would naturally make studies for his more important literary appearances, studies in subject-matter, as well as in verse and music. And a large number of his poems, at least considered in their entirety, must be thought of as compositions intended for courtly audiences.

It is to be presumed that Neidhart began by writing in the conventional style of the love-singers. But his sense of humor and his originality were too vigorous to allow him to continue in the polished and monotonous manners of the school that reached its acme in Reinmar. He possessed the creative faculty, and the rude village lyrics were a sufficient suggestion of the new departure that he at once instituted and consummated. He put in the place of lyrical elegies, lyrical snatches of epic; and instead of gathering his epic materials from the already familiar, even if not hackneyed, cycles of chivalry, he took them from the real life, and that a growing life, of the German villagers of his time. Their boorish manners and arrogant social pretensions, their vulgar assumptions of elegance, and their jealous, recklessly brutal tempers, he sketches vividly. His touch is not to be called magical, there are no imaginative hauntings about the poems, there is little fascination of subtle poetry in his expression or his melodies. But his rude subjects are by no means treated rudely; he shows excellent technique in those elaborately built stanzas; his tone rather deepens than shrills in excited movements: in his dash and energy of feeling, he retains artistic self-possession; while he is such an iconoclast of sentimental poetry, that some have thought that Walther had him in mind in his complaint of the new school. He invariably shows sentiment for nature in his preludes, as well as sympathetic tones for character, especially in what we may call his personal confessions. It is indeed by virtue of this combination of qualities, as well as by his novelty of subject, that he caught the approval of his age. Romantic idealism was dying out, and a long period of coarse sensibility was drawing on; while there was yet still some feeling for sentiment, and an intellectual appreciation of artistic performance was, as usual, lapping over the first stages of literary decadence. If we accept the view which I have suggested, that at least as wholes many of Neidhart's songs were intended only for the gentry, we may find it easier to meet the question of their autobiographic and actual significance.

It is possible to be unduly literal and too credulous of the historic reality of whatever is found in an old literature. Especially in the works of the minnesingers, some modern Germans appear unconscious that a poet may relate fictitious experiences and sensations. As I have remarked in an earlier essay, Cowley's love-poems had many mediæval prototypes, and there seems no necessity for assuming a fact behind each of Neidhart's statements. Why is it not reasonable to suppose that having once made what we call a "strike" with some of his village characters, he occasionally invented continuations or parallels? We may go so far as to assert the possibility that the continual reappearances of Engelmar, Neidhart's most recurrent character, who is always associated with the beginning of his disasters, is due quite as much to the fact that his early treatment of the famous snatching of a girl's mirror proved, by virtue of the topic, or the melody, or both, a great favorite, as to the incident in itself having been of the fateful influence upon his life that is implied. In other cases, as in what we may term the episode of the ginger-root, Neidhart certainly seems to be referring to some of his most popular earlier songs, for no other reason than that the reference would be agreeable to his audience and give a sort of continuity to his work. One of these instances is almost pathetic. The poet is old and song comes hard to him. After several stanzas of unusually serious tone, he says that people ask him why he does not sing as they are told he once did: they keep wondering what has become of the peasants who used to be on Tulnaere-field. So he attempts to conclude with a strain of his old satirical gaiety. "I'll tell of the bold free ways of Limizun, who is yet worse than our friend who took Friderun's mirror, or those who bought mail awhile ago at Vienna," as if by the mention of these popular achievements of his younger wit he could hide his dull present mood.

So, too, as it appears to me, we may explain the recurrent complaints of his unhappy loves and of his desires frustrated by one and another of the boors. These lover's sorrows are just what we should expect from a poet in Neidhart's relation to the fashionable love lyrics; he retains something of the tone of despondent yearning that was deemed requisite by all his predecessors, yet he gives it a piquant novelty by substituting irony and class animosities for vague and impersonal wailings, and the sense of humor in these courtly woes in behalf of mere peasant maidens would be a livelier attraction to the knights and ladies of his polite circles than we might suppose. Surely Neidhart was the victim of no deep passion for his rustic heroines. He may have been amused by them, or even have liked them, and he certainly was enraged at being interfered with or baffled by middle-class rivals; but his rôle is more a Lothario's than a true lass-lorn wooer's. Imagine a peasant farm-house with a large main apartment, such as Neidhart had in mind in one of his earliest winter songs: "Engelmar, thy room is good; chill is it in the dales: winter is hateful." The young farmers and the girls come trooping in by pairs and little groups, dressed in their best, smiling and gay: no better aid to imagining the scene could be desired than Defregger's genial picture of a modern Tyrolese peasant party. It is a change from the summer dances: "Winter, thy might will drive us indoors from the broad linden. Thy winds are cold. Lark, quit thy singing: both frost and snow have said thee nay; alas, for the green clover. May, to thee I am loyal; winter is my bane." "Winter gives joy to none but such as love the chimney-corner." They all think of the change from their summer gatherings, and the singer strums his fiddle and strikes into the nature prelude of his lyric, as they prepare to begin the dance. Here is another opening, translated in the stanza system of the original:

The green grass and the flowersBoth are gone;Before the sun the linden gives no shade;Those happy hoursOn shady lawnOf various joys are over; where we played,None may play;No paths strayWhere we went together;Joy fled away at the winter weather,And hearts are sad which once were gay.

We are reminded again of Herrick in his lines to the meadows:

"Ye have been fresh and green,Ye have been fill'd with flowers;And ye the walks have been,Where maids have spent their hours."

The dance is under way now; if, as sometimes happened, they paid a surprise visit, the guests have taken hold and made the room ready:

Clear out the benches and stools;Set in the middleThe trestles, then fiddle;We'll dance till we're tired, merry fools.Throw open the windows for air,That the breezeSoftly pleaseThe throat of each child debonair.When the leaders grow weary to sing,We'll all say,"Fiddler, playUs the tune for a stylish court-fling."

(They apparently piled the table-frames in the middle of the room in place of the linden, about which they danced on the lawn.)

The singer goes on to remind them of the preparation for the party:

"I advise my friends to consult where the children shall have their fun. Megenwart has a large room: if it like you all, we will have the holiday party there. His daughter wishes us to come. All of you tell the rest. Engelmar shall lead a dance around the table."

Again: "Let Kunegunde know; we shall be blamed if no one tells her about it, and don't forget Hedwig." Once more: "Come along, children, to the farm-house at Hademuot's; Engelbrecht, Adelmar, Friderich, Tuoze, Guote, Wentel, and her sisters all three; Hildeburg, pretty child; Jiutel and her cousin Ermelint."

Still again, in one of the cheerful early songs, before Neidhart's bitter tone came in:

> "Now for the children who've been asked to the party.
> Jiutel shall tell them all, that they are to step after the
> fiddle with Hilde. 'Twill be a great dance. Diemuot, Gisel,

are going together; Wendel, too, Engelmuot, for Heaven's sake! go out and call Künze to come.

"Tell her the man is here; if she cares to see him, as she has all the time been wishing to, let her put on a little jacket and her cloak; I should prefer to have her come here, than to have him find her there at home in her every day clothes.

"Künze tarried then no longer, but came, as Engelmuot bade her. She was in a hurry; quickly she dressed. Both sides of her gown were red silk. The finest of girls! No one could discover through the country, one I should be so glad to give my dear mother for a daughter.

"Haha! How she pleased me, when I saw what she was; such hair, and red lips. Then I asked her to sit by me, but she said: 'I don't dare; I've been told not to talk with you, or even sit by you. Go and ask Heilke over there by Vriderune!'"

"I hear dancing in the room," he sings at another time; "a crowd of village women are there; two fiddles; when they pause, gay outbreak of talking and laughing. Through the window goes the hubbub. Adelber never dances but between two girls." Sometimes the knightly guest entered into the gay interlude of conversation, entertaining a merry screaming group. But when his moody vein, or vexation at some common man's successful rivalry, dulled his social spirits, he would stand apart, or go to one side with one of the peasant maids, and satirically note the men scattered over the room. The young farmer's assumption of the dress and manners of gentility, carrying arms, discarding rustic fashions, affecting polite speech ("*Mit sîner rede er vlaemet*," Neidhart says of one of them,—he talks like a fine gentleman from abroad),—all this was ridiculous to the courtly poet, and his sense of the humor of it was associated with the bitterness of social contempt. "Look at Engelmar, how high he holds his head. What elegant style he has, at the dance, with his showy sword; something different from his father Batze. His son is a poor gawk, with his rough head. He puffs himself out like a stuffed pigeon, that sits crop-full on a corn-chest." And again: "Did you ever see so gay a peasant as he is? Good Lord! he is first of all in the dance. His sword-band is two hands broad. Proud enough he, of his new jacket; it has four and twenty small pieces of cloth in it, and the sleeves come down over his hand."[8] "There are two peasants wearing coats in the court style, of Austrian cloth. Uoze never cut them."

Then he goes on to say:

> "Perhaps you would like to hear how the rustics are dressed. Their clothes are above their place. Small coats they wear, and small cloaks; red hoods, shoes with buckles, and black hose. They have on silk pouch-bags, and in them they carry pieces of ginger, to make themselves agreeable to the girls. They wear their hair long, a privilege of good birth. They put on gloves that come up to their elbows. One appears in a fustian jacket green as grass. Another flaunts it in red. Another carries a sword long as a hemp flail, wherever he goes; the knob of its hilt has a mirror, that he makes the girls look at themselves in. Poor clumsy louts, how can the girls endure them? One of them tears his partner's veil, another sticks his sword hilt through her gown, as they are dancing, and more than once, enthusiastically dancing and excited by the music, their awkward feet tread on the girls' skirts and even drag them off. But they are more than clumsy, they have an offensive horse-play kind of pleasantry that is nothing less than insult. They put their hands in wrong places, and one of them tries to get a maiden's ring, and actually wrenches it from her finger as she is treading the bending *reie*.
>
> "Why should I not be angry at his insolence? Yet I would not mind the ring so much, if he had not hurt her hand."

And just so, Engelmar snatched her mirror from Neidhart's darling Vriderune.

This last, as has been said, is the most famous incident in the Neidhart story. From it he dates all his misfortunes, and he reverts to it, over and over, with bitterness that can hardly be regarded as merely ironical humor. Yet numerous as the references are, there is a mystery about the affair that has not been cleared up. It has been suggested that Vriderune's way of taking the rudeness made it clear to Neidhart that it was her peasant lover, and not himself, whom she really liked, but it would seem more natural to associate the occurrence with something violent. Possibly the poet's indignation at the boorish familiarity led him to a personal attack, just as in another connection he threatens to strike an obnoxious fellow, and the resulting quarrel may have been taken up by friends of both, with such serious consequences that various annoyances followed on their part, which he could only return by insulting hits in his songs. The chances are all in favor of the poet's having been a slighter man physically than these farm-workers, at one of whom he sneers for the sacks that ride on his neck, and there are suggestions in the pseudo-Neidhart poetry of his having had helpers to a revenge. In one of these imitations it is said that through Neidhart's injury thirty-two had their left legs cut off, an evident exaggeration of an earlier imitation, where the writer reminds his hearers of what happened to Engelmar for taking Vriderune's mirror, that he lost his left leg and had to go on crutches. Such violent fights are authentically reported at merrymakings of the time, and as the aristocratic leader of such a brawl, Neidhart no doubt would find his subsequent residence among the peasants uncongenial. Yet why should he manifest such reserve, at the same time that he mentions the subject so constantly, referring to it long after he has left Bavaria? Is it possible that his jealousy and hot blood drove him to some underhanded attack in some such way as that in which a brilliant restoration poet tried to punish a supposed injury? This ill reputation as an aristocrat equally insolent and treacherous, might follow him to Austria; he would hardly be pleased to acknowledge in his poem what he had done, while the constant references to his injury in the insult of Vriderune, and the misfortunes to himself which it caused may be regarded as half defensive attempts to excite sympathy instead of disapproval. So much for possible explanations of this curious literary enigma, out of which we may make too much; for, as I have already suggested, Neidhart may only be doing what novelists sometimes do when they repeat a popular hit in characterization. At any rate, Vriderune seems to have been lost to her upper-class lover, "and ever from that time I have had some new heart-sorrow."

Neidhart constantly reverts to the peasants' brutality and eagerness to fight. "Look out for a brutish fellow named Ber. He is tall and broad-shouldered; he scarcely can get in at the door. Fie, who brought him here? He is the nephew of Hildebolt of Bern, who was pounded by Williher." Lanze, again, "had got himself up for a champion, and thought nothing could resist him. He put underneath a coat of mail. Snarling like a bear he goes; so ugly is he, one were a child who withstood him." And of another: "He wears a sword that cuts like shears, and a good safety hat. Whoever you are, you may well keep out of his way. Villagers, look out for him; his sword is poisoned. It's a well-tempered Waidover, that sword of his."

With such village-warriors, no wonder that the parties did not always end cheerfully. With a resemblance to modern slang Neidhart tells how they threaten to put sunshine through each other. The lively episode of a quarrel over a rural gallant's presenting a young lady with a piece of ginger, Neidhart says he cannot describe in full, for he came away. But "each began screaming to his friends; one called loudly: 'Help, gossip Wezerant.' He must have been in great difficulty to scream so for help. I heard Hildebolt's sister shriek: 'Oh, my brother, my brother!'" Another dance ends with a milder disagreement. "Ruoprecht found an egg—'I ween the devil gave it to him'—and threatened to throw it. Eppe got mad, and dared him. Ruoprecht threw it at the top of his head, and it trickled down over him." Sometimes, evidently, peacemakers interfered, as they did in Frideliep's and Engelmar's disagreement about Gotelint, so that the rivals did not fight, though "just like two silly geese they went toward each other, all the rest of the day."

Like all of those poets, Neidhart, though he says "I" very often, lets us become but indifferent acquaintances. We read some of the mediæval lyrists without feeling sure that we detect a single genuine personal note; they had little of our modern sense of individuality. With Neidhart we fare better than with most; yet, after all, we are hardly sure that some of his personal confessions are not formally or humorously assumed. Yet of one trait we are left in no doubt, his strong German sense for the fatherland. With many other Bavarians, he went to Syria and Damietta on the crusade of 1217-1219, led by Leopold VII. of Austria, and he has left us two songs which, though certainly different enough from the deep religious feeling of such crusade lyrics as Hartmann's or Walther's, are unmistakably sincere. The first opens with the minnesinger's usual spring and love-lorn stanzas, but Neidhart soon drops conventionality with the exclamation, "For my song the foreign folk here do not care: ah, blessings on thee, Germany!" It reminds us of Walther: nothing is like the German home. He thinks of sending a messenger, not we notice, to some town or castle, but to that village where he left the loving heart from which his constancy never wavers, and to the dear friends over-sea.

> "Tell them from us all that they should quickly see us there, joyous enough, except for these wide waves. Bear my glad service to my mistress, dear to me before all ladies, and say to friends and kinsmen that I am well. If they inquire how things are going with us pilgrims, tell them, dear boy, what ill these foreign folk have wrought us. Haste thee, be swift; after thee assuredly shall I follow, quick as ever I may. God grant we may live to see the happy day of going home."

"We are all scarcely alive," he goes on; "the army is more than half dead. Ah, were I there! By my beloved gladly would I rest, in mine own place." "If I may only grow old with her!" he cries, and he breaks out impatiently against those who keep delaying through August, instead of moving westward. "Nowhere could a man be better off than at home, in his own parish."

At last the expedition, dissatisfied and worn, as the returning crusaders always were, are on the confines of the longed-for country. We can imagine the straggling company making their way along, their minstrel riding among them, fingering the old violin that he has carried over his shoulders all the two years, and thinking out a new song. He is still a young man, or at least only approaching middle age, and thoughts of home, friendship, love, and the spring gaiety of the village life, crowd upon him with buoyant thrills; he strikes the strings more firmly, and his voice rings out a home-coming lyric, full of life and feeling. "The long bright days are come again, and with them the birds; it is a long time since they sang so well. The winter-weary are gayer than they have been for thirty years. Maidens, ye children, fine people all, let your hearts be free to the summer joy, spring quickly in the carols."

Dear herald, homeward go;'Tis over, all my woe;We're near the Rhine!

Neidhart's poems are readily classified in two divisions, his songs for summer and for winter. Both were probably sung as an accompaniment to the dances, either of the peasants or of the upper class, though there may be some doubt whether this is true of all the winter songs. Almost invariably he opens with a nature-prelude, often an elaborate one, and the temper of the songs is always congenial to the season, gay for summer, and gloomy or critical for winter.

There is no evidence that the difficulty with Engelmar was the occasion of the poet's leaving Bavaria, but his unpopularity with the peasants seems to have had something to do with the loss of his fief. He was cast down at the thought of parting with Reuenthal, and said that he would sing no longer, since the name under which his merry lines had been known was taken from him; and with a play on the word, "I am put out undeservedly, my friends; now leave me free of the name!" But after he was settled by Frederich on an Austrian fief, he adapted himself cheerfully to his new home. "Here I am at Medelicke, in spite of them all. I am not sorry that I sang so much of Eppe and of Gumpe at Reuenthal."

The Duke gave him money and a house, in response to musical solicitations, and Neidhart appealed for exemption from his heavy taxes, that threatened to consume what his children needed. With our modern ideas this system of literary patronage upon which mediæval poets depended, and which usually required direct and even pressing solicitation, seems painful to self-respect; we forget how lately it flourished. In those days when princely giving was an established custom, and differed from a system of salaries mainly in being a less regularly appointed income, a poet's request for a gift was scarcely more than a modern author's reminder of an unpaid claim; there is nothing of the unmanly dependence of Coleridge in these earlier suppliants for aid. None of them asked more gracefully—even Chaucer is not more delicately suggestive—than Neidhart in such lines as these:

> "Whoever had a bird who satisfied him with song through the year, he would occasionally look to his bird-cage, and give him good food. Then the bird could go on singing sweet melodies. If he always sang well to meet the May, he should be well cared for, summer and winter. Even the birds appreciate kind treatment."

But the times were bad, and even a box of silver, and a house to put it in, and remission of taxes, could not keep the poet gay as he passed into later life. He composed penitential lyrics, after orthodox precedents, of the love-singers, for they almost always grew old seriously. On these we need not linger, though there seems a cry fuller than the echo-note in his farewell to Lady Earth, and appeal for pardon for some of his foolish songs: "Lord God of Heaven, give me thy guidance; Might of all Might, now strengthen my heart, that I may win soul's health, and partake ever-enduring joy, through thy sweet will." But the wail of all of the thirteenth-century's serious minds, that things were going "ever the lenger the wers" in Christendom, comes out nowhere more deeply than in Neidhart's allegorical love-song to Joy of the World, chiding her for her change of character during his long, unrequited service:

> "False, shameless folk nowadays people her court, and her old household, truth, chastity, good manners, none find these any longer. My lady's honor is lame all over. She is fallen so that none can rescue her. She lies in such a pool that only God can make her clean. Men of wise mind be on your guard before her, in church or on street: women of worth keep far away."

Eighty new melodies he has sung in her service; this is the last, and not the most joyous.

To this closing period we may refer a few summer songs that are an exception to the usually light-hearted verses of that form. Their seriousness is all the more noticeable from their fair-weather setting; for once, the spring is not a panacea. "A delightful May has come, but alas, neither priest nor layman rejoices in its arrival. Were it the Emperor who had come, we might rejoice. Trouble and sorrow dwell in Austria." There is something here besides a sense that the joyousness of simple free-living and the loyalty of love-service are passing away; he attributes much of the social decline to national confusion and the political unrestraint. Yet controversial as he is in social relations, he has little of Walther von der Vogelweide's thoughtfulness and energy in patriotic polemics. He drifts down the stream with a sigh.

In the poem which Meyer's elaborate study of the order of his work places last, though only conjecturally, he again considers his friends' entreaty for more songs. The world goes too sadly, he says; as he had said before that they must ask Troestelin to sing; he himself had no longer a heart for poetry. Yet there is one pleasant story that he can tell them: "to break down troubles comes one worthy to be praised; 'tis May, with all his might." There is something pathetic in such songs, that try to assume the cheerful strain in which the poet, now grown gloomy, wrote while he was young. They remind us of the stray leaves that we sometimes see caught up to their old home among the branches by a sudden March gust; the brown leaves that will never again uncrumple their green infancies, hover for a moment, then sink hesitatingly back to the ground. In this one song, the nature stanzas are transferred from the place of prelude to the conclusion. "May has conquered; wood and heath have adorned themselves with their lovely attire; blue flowers are here and the roses," and he ends with the old thought, that joyousness and virtuous honor go together. As an idle fancy it is "pleasant if one consider it," to regard these as the final words of this knightly singer of mediæval country scenes, the last of the great figures of that old German group, a parting reminder of the philosophy of a happy life which mediæval lyrists often maintained so earnestly,—that the secret of good living is blitheness of heart, and out-of-door life in spring and summer. For many of these old poets the two terms were convertible; their creed was surely a simple one.

MEIER HELMBRECHT,

A GERMAN FARMER OF THE THIRTEENTH CENTURY.

The usual conception of the middle ages seems to consist of a few facts and theories about the feudal system and the crusades, the names with possibly some traits of a few eminent public figures and a general impression of confusion and obscurity. Supplementing this central idea, one usually sees a panel picture on either side. One, sunshine flashing from the spears and armor of knights tilting in tournaments, and watched by dimly beautiful women; in the distance a solitary knight pricking over a plain, or, guided by the wail of an unseen and lovely captive, making his way through forest haunts of giants and gnomes. The other, a lowering twilight overhanging gloomy monastery walls, the shelter of melancholy, hypocrisy, manuscript illuminations, and a barren, difficult philosophy. Sunshine and twilight on either hand, and in the background an impenetrable mist concealing the great masses of humanity, as well as all concrete actual lives even of the great. A little information and a little romance are unsatisfactory artists for a sketch of mediævalism. We soon discover that there is a great deal behind such a picture of soldiers living in wars, and in the tourneying pretence of war; or schoolmen contending in brilliant logical panoply within and without spectral philosophic fastnesses; or hermits, nuns, and monks fighting against God's present that they might win His future; or marauders beating down helplessness and innocence.

Yet we may study the middle ages laboriously, and find ourselves still confronted by the mist that hangs over the rank and file. Our curiosity about these forgotten multitudes teases us. "How is it that you lived, and what is it that you did?" we ask these distant prototypes of Wordsworth's peasant. We come to discover that there is much behind our slight old notion of chivalry and monasticism; though seven hundred years have changed its conditions, life then and now is yet less different than we had thought. But we find it difficult to acquire much information about those social substrata on which the learned and the polite classes rested. Clio is the most aristocratic of the ladies nine, and that instinct of vitality whereby we count fame for ourselves something desirable, makes us think with a certain compassion of great armies of those generations filing sullenly on, not only as individuals, but as whole masses, to the grave of oblivion. The little that we know makes us sure only that they were wretched, their lives the most gloomy of all the lives of gloomy ages.

We may read thousands of pages of the literature of those days with scarcely any addition to our knowledge of the work-a-day world, for most of the poetry is romantic, and in its imitative phases mainly a reflection of courtly customs and character. The middle ages in Germany and France were anything but uncivilized, and the poetry of secondary cultivation is, as was said in the last essay, likely to prefer idealistic interpretation of its finest development to democratic realism. Yet the student finds from time to time interesting material for an account of the average life, and in the poet whom this essay is designed to introduce to a modern audience, we obtain an extended study in this side field of literary interpretation. He wrote not of high life but of the middle classes, not in romance but in a literal yet at the same time artistic manner that we may call a heightened realism. He appears to have been himself one of the people, a poet who possibly made his living by reciting poems of incident, and by singing at their merrymakings, though of this there is no evidence. It has been thought by some German scholars that he may have been a monk, but the indications make rather against than for this view. We know in fact nothing whatever about him except for one single line, in which he tells us that his name is Wernher the Gardener.

As was said, his poem is remarkable as being the heightened treatment of a plain story of the peasant classes a little before 1250; it is remarkable, too, for the liveliness and simple force of his treatment. He is an artist—though he works in chalks instead of water-colors;—unornamented, unassuming, he produces an impression of personal power, moral seriousness, a clear eye for what he saw, and the power to state it directly, one of the marks of a later and more developed age. He has no little dramatic liveliness, a sense of humor, and the pleasantest love for the plain beauties of character and home-life.

He tells the story of a farmer, Helmbrecht, and his wayward son. The boy has been the admiration of his peasant family as the oldest child, notable for his splendid yellow hair, and full of life and spirit. At the time the poem opens he has grown to early manhood, dissatisfied with the hidden and laborious life of tiller of the soil, vain of his appearance, fond of fine dress, and ambitious to live easily and be admired. He is petted and indulged by his mother and his sister Gotelint, and when he desires a hood—a part of masculine costume much affected by gallant youths—they provide him with one so fine that it becomes famous far and near. Embroidery, as every one knows who is acquainted with the mediæval arts, was the most artistic accomplishment of the period. Ladies learned to embroider and weave the most complicated and elaborate devices; handicraftsmen of all sorts put on their work representations so copious that one sometimes wonders whether the literary descriptions of them are not exaggerations. Can the frequency and detail of these passages, we wonder, be a faintly remembered tradition of the devices put by Homer on the shield of Achilles, or by Vergil on the gates of the rising Carthage? At any rate, tapestries, cloths, and garments, to say nothing of saddles and the like, were covered by picture after picture, in almost every important poem of the age. This young peasant Helmbrecht's hood was embroidered, not, of course, by the rude country fingers of his mother and sister, but by a clever nun, who had run away from her nunnery to enjoy the pleasures of a lively youth. Many were the wages of farm-produce by which she was persuaded to fit out the young man. The hood was covered with birds, parrots, and doves; on one side were representations of the siege of Troy and the escape of Æneas; on the other, the stout deeds of Charlemagne, Roland, and Oliver, in their wars against the heathen Moors. Behind, adventures of old German legendary heroes, in the cycle of Dietrich of Bern. In front, dances of knights, ladies, and of maidens and young esquires—the favorite and mediæval dance, where the gentleman stood between two ladies, holding the hand of each.

After this acquisition the boy became ambitious for still more finery, and was indulged in an elaborate costume that need not be described. Such white linen, such a splendid blue coat, all covered with buttons, gilded ones in double rows down the back, around the collar, and in front of silver. About the shoulders little bells were hung, that rang merrily when he sprang in the *reie*. Ah, very love-lorn were the glances cast on him by women and girls at the dance.

At last he is fully equipped by the love and sacrifice of his family, and they are happy in his elegance, and contented with themselves because the self-willed and capricious boy is pleased; when suddenly the simple household is thrown into grief and anxiety by his announcement that he is going to leave home. He must have a horse—there was none on the farm—to complete his outfit as a gentleman, and then he will ride away to some court and seek his fortune. In vain they remonstrate.

> "'My dear father, help me on. My mother and sister have helped me so that I shall love them all my life.'

> "His father was troubled to hear that he was resolved to go, but he said to him: 'I'll give you a fast horse for your outfit, good at hedges and ditches, for you to have there at court. I'll buy him for you willingly, if I can find one for sale. But, my dear son, now give up going to court. The ways there are hard for those who have not been used to them from the time they were children. My dear son, now drive team for me, or if you'd rather, hold the plough, and I'll drive for you, and let us till the farm, so you'll come to your grave full of honors like me; at least I hope to, for I

surely am honest and loyal, and every year I pay my tithes. I have lived my life without hate and without envy.'

"But the son replied: 'My dear father, keep quiet and stop talking; there's only one way about it, I'm going to find out how things smack there at court. Your sacks sha'n't load my back any longer. I won't load any more manure on your wagon, and God hate me if I ever yoke oxen for you again, and sow your oats. That's not the thing for my long yellow hair and my curly locks, and my close-fitting coat, and my fine hood, and the silk doves the women worked on it. I won't help you farm any longer.'

"'Dear son, stay with me. I am certain that farmer Ruoprecht will give you his daughter, with lots of sheep and swine, and ten cattle, old and young. At court you'll be hungry, you'll have to lie hard, and give up all comforts. Now take my advice, and it will be to your interests and credit. It very seldom happens that a man gets along well who rebels against his own station. Your station is the plough. My son, I swear to you that the genuine court-people will make fun of you, my dear child. Do as I say, and give it up.'

"'Father, if I only have a horse I shall get on as well in the court ways as those who were born there. Any one who saw that hood on my head would swear a thousand oaths that I never worked for you, or drove a plough through a furrow. Whenever I put on the clothes my mother and my sister gave me yesterday, I sha'n't look much as if I ever took a flail to thresh wheat on the barn floor, or as if I ever drove stakes. When I get my legs and my feet in the hose and cordovan boots, nobody'll know that I ever made fence for you or any one else. Let me have a horse, and farmer Ruoprecht may go without me for a son-in-law. I'll not give up my future for a wife.'"

The father goes on pleading with the boy to take advice and keep out of the disorderly life he is likely to get into about a court. By the silent assumption that his new master and his people will pillage from the peasantry, we get a suggestion of the lawlessness of the country—which had grown worse during the long absenteeism of Frederic II. But if the peasants catch you, he tells his son with energy, you will fare much worse than one of the gentlemen would. They will take the quickest revenge, and think that they are doing God service when they find one of their own kind stealing.

But the son only goes on to repeat that he will leave the farm. He talks just as an ambitious country fellow will talk to-day about the slow life and small profits. He becomes bolder and more insolent. If it were not for that wretched horse he would be riding with the rest across fields and dragging peasants through the hedges; the cattle would be lowing as he drove them off. He says he can endure poverty no longer;—raising a colt or an ox for three years, and then selling them for just nothing. So his father traded a large piece of homespun, four good cows, two oxen, three steers, and four bushels of wheat,—all worth about ten pounds,—for a horse that could not have been sold for three ("alas for the wasted seven!"), and the young man put on his finery, tossed his head, and, looking around, jauntily declared that he could "bite through a stone, or eat iron, he felt so fierce." If he could catch the Emperor or the Duke, there would be some money coming in. "'Father, you could manage a Saxon easier than me.'"

When he calls upon his father to release him from the family control, the latter assents, though with all his old reluctance. Indeed he cannot let him go without one more appeal:

> "'I give you your liberty, my son. But take care that no one yonder hurts your hood and its silk doves, or viciously tears your long yellow hair. And I am afraid that at the end you will be following a staff, or some little boy will be leading you.'"

Then once more, after a pause, comes the abrupt:

> "'My son, my own dear boy, give up going. You shall live on what I live, and on what your mother gives you. Drink water, my dear son, before you steal to buy wine. Austrian pie, any one, fool or wise man, will tell you, is food fit for gentlemen. Eat that, dear child, instead of giving an ox you have stolen to some inn-keeper for a chicken. Your mother can cook good broth; eat that, instead of giving a stolen horse for a goose. My son, mix rye with oats sooner than eat fish in a dishonored life. If you will not obey me, go. But though you win wealth and great honors, never will I share them with you. And misfortune—have that alone too.'

> "'You drink water, father, but I'll drink wine. Eat your mush, but I'll eat what they call fricasseed chicken there and white wheat bread; oats will do for you. They say at Rome that a child takes after his godfather, and mine was a knight. Thank God for giving me such high and noble ideas.'"

But the old farmer replied that he liked much better a man who did right and remained constant to it.

> "Even though his birth might be rather humble, he would please the world better than a king's son without virtue and honor. An honest man of lowly rank, and a nobleman who was not courteous and honorable,—let the two come to a land where neither is known, and the child of lowly birth will outrank the high-born. My son, if you will be noble, on my word I counsel you, do noble deeds. Good life is a crown above all nobility."

There is the old thought, so common in literature from ancient authors down to the poet of Lady Clara Vere de Vere, and especially a favorite with writers of the middle age. Possibly some of them caught it from Boëthius, who expressed it more than once in the testament of wise and generous character that he left to the world from his confinement at Pavia, and that proved so singularly congenial to the mediæval mind; but we need certainly not require the aid of origins to account for its frequency. Aristocratic as many phases of the times were, there were a number of important evening influences, conspicuously two: the church, in whose monastery cloisters the rich and poor met together as brothers of one impartial discipline, and from whose ranks members of low birth might rise to be the peers of dukes; and the orders of chivalry, which received approved squires from the middle class. Thus, in addition to aristocracy of birth, there was a conditional gentility to which those who had the claim of merit might aspire. But though the thought that desert, and not descent, is the test for nobility, is so obvious in the days when position carried with it so strong a connotation of power, and when the upper strata of society bore down so hard and haughtily upon the lower, we always feel satisfaction in coming upon a trim statement of the fine old commonplace whose best mediæval expression we can quote from a poet of our own language:

"Look, who that is moost vertuous alway,Pryvee and apert, and moost entendeth ayTo do the gentil dedes that he kan,Taak hym for the grettest gentil man."

"'Alas, that your mother bore you!'" the farmer exclaimed, when the boy's only answer to his appeal was to declare his hair and hood better fitted for a dance than for the plough or the harrow. "'Thou wilt leave the best and do the worst'"; and he goes on to contrast the man who lives against God and the good of others, followed by every one's curses, with the man who helps the world along, trying night and day to do good by his life, and thereby honors God. This one, wherever he may turn, has the love of God and all the world.

> "'Dear son,' he says, 'that man you might be, if you would yield to me. Till with the plough, and plenty of people will be the better for your life, poor and rich; nay, even wolf and eagle, and everything that lives on earth. Many a woman must be made more beautiful through the farmer, many a king must be crowned through the produce of the farm. Indeed, there is no one so noble that his pride would not be a very small thing, except for the farmer.'"

How natural all this sounds,—agriculture the basis of society, tillage of the soil alike useful and honorable. With what quiet manliness this old German talks of the dignity of labor, with no touch of the modern arrogance and discontent with the existing social condition. He will keep to his rank in life, and be loyal to his station, yet, though he looks up with a simple-hearted interest and wonder to the great world above him, he reflects as he follows his plough that without him that great world's pride "would be a very small thing." But there is a quality here that is still finer: the undercurrent perception of "the gospel of service." It is not only that honesty is the best policy, though the peasant is shrewd, and appreciates the practical side too; his conversation with the boy breathes the best nineteenth-century spirit of the duty of making one's life valuable to others. That sentence about working night and day to be useful, and thereby honoring God, is no commonplace for our century, to say nothing of the thirteenth. There is something pretty, too, in the touch of sympathy with the animal world; in some way, he feels that even the birds and beasts must be better off for a good farmer.

These times seem often savage in their cruelties and recklessness of giving pain, but they have a gentle side as well, as may be seen in the tales cited by Montalembert of friendly relations between monks and wild beasts, and in examples collected by Uhland in his essay on the old German animal literature. It is pleasant in connection with such barbarities as we shall presently be reminded of in this very poem to recall the myth versified by Longfellow, of the great minnesinger's legacy to the monastery, conditioned on the brethren's every day placing grain and water for the birds upon his grave; and more than one authentic story is told like that of the Abbot of Hirsan, who, when snow was deep in winter, would take oats from his barn to feed the birds.

After the young Helmbrecht has begged God to release him soon from his father's preaching,—"if you only had been a real preacher you might have got up a whole army with your sermons for a crusade,"—and has explained that instead of keeping on ploughing, he is resolved to have white hands, and no longer need to feel mortified whenever he holds ladies' hands at a dance, his father resorts to his last resource—an appeal to superstition, that he has been keeping in reserve. He tells him what he has been dreaming—three dreams that he interprets as ominous of the loss of sight, feet, and arms, and worst of all, a final dream of one of those sights so common for many centuries before and after, but made no less dreadful by familiarity.

> "'You were hanging on a tree. Your feet were a fathom from the ground. Above your head on a bough sat a raven, by its side a crow. Your hair was all tangled. On the right hand the raven combed your head for you, on the left the crow.'"

But the hopeful rode gaily off through the bars, and came to a castle where a warlike lord was glad to receive any addition to his force. There he stayed for a year, leading the extreme bandit life of whose outrages and oppressions we read so much during this troubled period. He quickly obtained reputation as daring and merciless:

> "Into his sack he stuffed everything; it was all one to him. Nothing was too small, nothing too great. Helmbrecht took it all, rough and smooth, crooked and straight. He took horses, cattle, jacket, sword, cloak, coat, goats, sheep. From women he stripped everything, and well enough his ship went that first year, 'its sails full.' But after a while, as people are wont to think of going home, he took leave of the court, and commended them to the good God."

They heard at the farm that he was coming on for a visit, and in accordance with the ancient custom of giving a present to the bearer of good news, the messenger received a shirt and pair of hose. But when the young man himself arrived, "how he was received! Did they step forward to meet him? Nay, they ran, all together; one crowded past another; father and mother sprang as if they had never had a care." It is touching to notice the suggestiveness of a single line in the poet's description of the scene. The plain people understood that their son was no longer one of them, and they knew how his earlier false pride must have grown in this year's absence in the outer world. So in their anxiety that everything should gratify this brilliant, wayward eldest son of their admiration and hope, and that nothing should interfere with his being pleased and gracious to their yearning, timid love, and knowing how in the homely heartiness of their joy at seeing their young master again the two servants would treat him at once in the old familiar way of peasant-farm equality, they instructed their man and their woman in what they thought to be polite salutation. So when the guest appeared, "Did the woman and the man cry 'Welcome back, Helmbrecht'? Nay, they did not; they had been told not to. They said: 'Master, in God's name be you welcome.'" There is a touch of humor in their rushing forward and being the first to greet him, in their rude good-feeling; but we also get a sense of tenderness from seeing the father and mother keeping in the background, behind their daughter Gotelint.

Little education as there was in the middle ages, people fully appreciated the elegance as well as the utility of a knowledge of foreign languages, and no accomplishment was held more desirable. Especially the Germans, representing an outlying civilization, would send their sons, while still boys, to some French court to serve as pages and acquire especially the language as well as other branches of knightly culture. The praises of various heroes of French as well as German romances, give to linguistic attainments a high place; Gottfried, for example, in his account of the training of Tristan, who was the typical gentleman of the romances, says that from the age of seven until he was fourteen he was studying languages under the care of a tutor, by travelling through different lands. Since this was the fashion, imitations were sure to become popular, and a thin veneering of foreign speech became the mark of a pinchbeck culture, just as it has been so frequently since. Accordingly, after the servants have cried out their "Master, in God's name be you welcome," and Gotelint has thrown her arms about her brother, the young gallant calls her his dear little sister in a phrase of salutation touched with Low Dutch, which he follows by the elegant "gratia vester." Then the younger children ran up, and last of all the farmer and his wife, who greeted him over and over. He addressed his father in French: "Deu sal"; his mother in Bohemian: "Dobraytra." They looked at each other; four strange languages all together—there must be some mistake.

> "The housewife said: 'My dear, this is not our son. This is a Bohemian or a Slav.' Her husband replied: 'It is a Frenchman. My son whom I commended to God, certainly this is not he, and yet he looks like him.' And Gotelint suggested: 'He answered me in Latin; may be he is a priest.' 'Faith,' put in the hired man, who had caught the phrase in dialect, 'he has lived in Saxony or Brabant, for he said, "liebe susterkindekin"; he must be a Saxon.'"

The old peasant was devoted and loving, but he had resolution and self-respect under it all. He told the accomplished youth that before he would take him for his son he must talk German. If he would do that and declare himself Helmbrecht, well and good. He should have a chicken boiled, and another roasted, and his horse should be well cared for. But a Bohemian, or a Slav, or a Saxon, or a Brabanter, or a Frenchman, or a priest, should be given nothing. The youth began to reflect. It was getting late, there was no place near by where he could go; so he concluded to waive his elegant manners, and speak in the old style. But the shrewd peasant feigns incredulity, and decides to test his son a little further. In vain the young man protests himself Helmbrecht. His gentility must stoop to vulgar peasant identification, and tell what he knows about the oxen on the farm. He rattles over all four of them, Grazer, Black-spot, Rascal, and White-star, with a little praise for two, and the reconciliation is accomplished. Thereupon the repressed fondness and devotion obtain free expression. The father hurried out to attend to the horse, the mother sent her daughter for a pillow and cushion—"Run, now, and don't walk for it"—and makes a couch for him on the bench close to the stove, so that he may have a nap while she is preparing his dinner. When the boy woke the meal was ready, and Wernher assures us that any gentleman might have enjoyed it. After washing his hands, the usual first step in a meal, a dish of fine-cut sauerkraut was put before him, by it bacon, both fat and lean, and a rich mellow cheese. Then there was as fat a goose as ever roasted on a spit—and with what good-will they provided that extraordinary peasant luxury—a roasted and a boiled chicken. A knight out hunting, and happening on such a meal, would like it well. For besides this they had managed to get delicacies in which peasants never think of indulging. "'If I had any wine you should be drunk to-night,'" the farmer said; and he added—with such a noble union of dignity, simplicity, and sentiment for the plain homely blessings which he had appreciated and loved all his life: "'My dear son, now take a drink of water from the best spring that ever came out of earth. I know no spring fit to be compared with it, except the one at Wankhûsen.'"

"'Tell me, son,'" he continued, as they went on with their dinner, for he could not wait to ask him, "'tell me how about the court fashions, and then I will tell you how they used to be when I was young.'" But the son was too busy eating to stop to talk then, and he allowed his father to relate his early reminiscences.

> "'When I was a boy,' he began 'and your grandfather Helmbrecht had sent me to court with cheese and eggs, just as a farmer does to-day, I took note of the knights, and marked their ways. They were courteous and cheerful and had no rascality about them in those days, such as many men and women too have now. The knights had a custom, to make themselves pleasing to the ladies, that was called jousting. A man of the court explained it to me when I asked him what they called it. Two companies would come together from opposite directions, riding as if they were mad, and they would drive against each other, as if their spears must pierce through. There's nothing in

these days like what I saw then. After that they had a dance, and while dancing they sang lively songs, that made the time go quickly. Presently a playman came forward and struck in with his fiddle; at that the ladies jumped up, and the knights went to meet them, and they took hold of hands. That was a pleasant sight—the overflowing delight of ladies and gentlemen, dancing so gaily, poor and rich. When that was over a man came out and read about some one called Ernest. Each could do whatever he liked. Some took their bows and shot at a target; others went hunting: there was no end to the kinds of pleasure. The worst off there would be the best off with us now. Those were the times before false and vicious people could turn the right about with their tricks. Nowadays the wise man is the one who can cheat and lie; he has position and money and honor at court, much more than the man who lives justly and strives after God's grace.'"

We find here as in so many other places in thirteenth century poetry, that the serious-minded were already looking back. Just as we have seen Walther and Ulrich bewailing the lost sunshine of chivalry, Wernher laments that the old-time honesty has gone, and with it the knightly light-hearted honorable joys. Already, before 1250, there was a halo about the chivalric court; ladies were honored, knights tourneyed for their pleasure; dancing with them attracted gentlemen quite beyond drinking bouts; the poet's narratives of old German heroes were yet in fashion.

All this seems amusing to the young man; what sappy and goody-goody fashions those were. He thinks it manly to swagger about the new ways, and tell how the fashionable cry is "Trinkà, herre, trinkà trinc!" It used to be good breeding to dangle about pretty ladies, but the correct thing now is just to drink. "'This is the kind of love-letters we have: "You dear little barmaid, fill up our cups. What a fool a man is who wastes his life for women, instead of good wine." It's a genteel thing to be sharp with your tongue, and get the best of people, and tell clever lies.'"

The old man hears, and with a sigh wishes back the day when gentlemen shouted "Heyā, ritter, wis et frō!" in the tourneys, instead of these new cries of riotry and pillage. The son would tell him more, but he has ridden far and wishes to go to sleep. There were no linen sheets in that farm-house, but Gotelint spread a newly washed shirt on his bed, and he slept until high day. The next morning he displayed the gifts he had brought: for his father, a whetstone, scythe, and axe; for his mother, a fox-skin; for Gotelint, a head-dress with a band of silk and gold, better fitted for a nobleman's child than for her; shoes with straps for the farm-hand; and for his wife, a cloth to cover her hair, and a red ribband. He remained at home for a week, and then he became restless to return. His father again took up his entreaties, begging him in the tenderest tones to stay from the bitter and sour life he has been leading. As long as he lives he will share what he has with him, even if the young man will do nothing but sit still and wash his hands. Only he must not go back.

What, not go back with so much to do? Has not a rich man ridden over the field of his god-father? Has not another rich man eaten bread with crullers? And still a third, while eating at a bishop's table, loosened his girdle? Each one must be taught better manners through wholesale plunder of cattle, sheep, and swine, to say nothing of a boor who blew the foam off his beer. He and some friends will give them a good training, and he runs over the list of his bandit companions with the cant names borne by each, such as Lambswallow, Hellbag, Bolt-the-sheep, Coweater, Wolfthroat, and at last his own name, Swallow-the-land.

We may pass by the exploits of which he boasts—the children of the peasants near him eat water-gruel, their father's eyes he puts out, their beards he draws with pincers, he binds them in ant-hills, or smokes them in the chimney, and so forth, through a revolting list of barbarities.

The youth uncloaks himself as a full-fledged desperado, and his father's short, stern warning in God's name of vengeance only throws him into a passion, and he declares that, though hitherto on their raids he has kept off his companions from the farm, instead of doing so longer, he will give up his father and mother to their will. He reveals what had been a main motive in his visit, an arrangement he had made with his comrade Lambswallow to let him marry Gotelint. But of that brilliant match her father's conduct has deprived the girl; also she will never find another man who can give her such luxuries of dress and fare. Moreover, his sister was worthy of such a husband, and he stops to repeat the tribute he had paid to her while discussing the alliance with his friend. The lines bring before us a weird mediæval scene, to which these reckless free-livers looked forward as their assured end, and which they dreaded most from the lurid light thrown by superstition upon the picture. The ghastly swinging of their corpses on the gibbet ("The rain has drenched and washed us," Villon says two hundred years later, "and the sun dried and blackened us. Magpies and crows have hollowed out our eyes, and plucked away our beards and eyebrows."[9]) troubled them less than the thought that their falling bones must lie unburied, and their lives be followed by no religious rites to mitigate the eternal justice. French poetry has interpreted this phase of crime and misery in Villon's *Epitaphe*; in English it has been interpreted by Tennyson in *Rizpah*, at once the most intense and the most piteous of all his poems, as free from self-consciousness as an early ballad, the most pathetic expression in all literature of a mother's love, and kept out of the category of the very greatest poems only by the intolerable anguish of its emotion. In this old German story we find an interpretation of it too; the briefest and much the simplest, yet not without an unobtrusive power. Young Helmbrecht declares that he told his comrade that he might trust Gotelint never to make him repent his choice.

> "I know her," he represents himself as saying, "to be so loyal—on this you may count—that she never will leave you hanging long; she will cut you down with her own hands, and carry you to your grave at the cross-roads, with incense and myrrh—of this you can be sure. Nightly for a whole year she will go about you. Or if, less fortunate, you are blinded or crippled by the loss of hands or feet, the good, pure girl will guide you with her own hand over all the paths of every land; every morning she will bring your crutches to your bed, or cut for you, even till you die, your bread and meat."

From the first, Gotelint has been under the fascination of her brother, and as she hears his long account of the life the wife of Lambswallow must live, she calls young Helmbrecht aside, and arranges to run away from home and marry his friend. So at the appointed time she does, and a great wedding feast, provided at the cost of many widows and orphans, follows the curious mediæval marriage ceremony. In the midst of it a strange foreshadowing of evil comes over her; she wishes herself back at her father's simple fare; his cabbage was better than the luxury of Lambswallow's fish. She tells her bridegroom that she is afraid strangers are at hand to harm them, and even as the players are receiving their gifts, the sheriff and his force break in upon the revellers. All meet quick justice; nine are hung; Helmbrecht, the tenth, is sent off blind, and with only one foot and one hand. "What the forsaken bride suffered" let him tell who saw.

The story works to its conclusion in a temper better fitted to the thirteenth century than to ours. The poet feels no complaisance for an obstinate wrong-doer. He says: "God is a worker of wonders, and this is the proper lot of a youth who called his father an old peasant and his mother a worthless woman." Nor does he stop with his own exclamation; he tells in detail how the blind and maimed fellow is brought by a boy to the farm, only to receive his father's taunts and mocking. Brutal and distressing as the passage seems, it is true to the age and to the character of the sturdy old farmer. While there was hope he had borne every insult; he had pleaded persistently, tenderly, and to every limit of generosity and devotion. But when the youth had proved himself susceptible to no claims of virtue or humanity, and, as a last stroke of evil, had seduced his sister from an honorable life, further pity seems sentimentalism. Before the boy's first departure his father had warned him that he would take no part in any ill-won prosperity, and if misfortunes came, they, too, must be borne alone. The foreign phrases are on the father's lips this time, as the sightless cripple creeps up to the farm-house door. He runs over the proud speeches that have thus ended in shame and misery; nor will he listen to the entreaties for shelter, even as a beggar, for a single night. "'Every one, the country round, is cruel to me; alas! so you are now. In God's name give me the charity you would give a poor sick man!'" But the farmer "laughed scoffingly, even though it broke his heart, for this was his own flesh, his child, who stood there before him blind." He struck the boy who was leading the wretch, and drove them off. "Yet as they went away his mother put a loaf of bread in his hand, as if he were a child." For a year he crawled about, skulking in the woods and living on what he might. Then one day, having wandered to the scene of some of his worst crimes, a set of peasants catch sight of him, and recount to one another what their farms, their babes, their daughters, had suffered from this outlaw and his band. As they talk they tremble with hate and rage, and, catching up a rope, they fulfil the last of the dreams that tormented the anxious night of the father just before his son rode out, with his rich clothes and fine horse and wonderful hood covering that long, beautiful hair, to seek his fortune in a court.

Why is it worth while to introduce to English readers this peasant tale of the middle ages? Not on account of its antiquarian value, though it is full of interesting suggestions of old manners. Nor primarily on account of its literary significance, notwithstanding the tact and nervous directness of Wernher's style, and the heightened realism of treatment that gives him distinction beside the romanticists of the time. Its main importance for us lies in that sense of the human unity which we derive from such a story of a time so remote from our own, and in most of its aspects so different. Many of the influences that render man's life desirable—organized society, with respect for property and personal safety, ease of living, humanitarian sensibility even to the guiltiest suffering—we miss, and missing them we rejoice in the progress of our age toward the light. But the traits whereby life in all ages becomes estimable—simplicity of character, contentment with the station of one's birth, if only one can live there with dignity and usefulness; frugality, integrity, natural love which grows most tender and yearning when the kinship of moral worthiness seems in danger of dissolution—are our own best possession, and this identity of manhood then and now makes us feel less strange among those distant and dimly remembered generations. Thus serious writers offer to our study many notable and interesting thoughts, and in their courtly poets we find scores of delightful pictures of gracious and noble dames and knights moving through the pleasures and pains of an ideal world. It is also pleasant to listen to a poet from among the people, and to touch the rough hand of an old German farmer, whose most brilliant recollection was of the time when, as a boy, he carried eggs and cheese to one of the courts of old-fashioned chivalry; whose virtue cast in a decadent era had looked at life sternly, yet whose austerity was softened by a homely simplicity through whose grace he grew old, with his heart true to his plain home life and his family, even to the assurance that no drink could be more refreshing than water from the spring on his own farm.

CHILDHOOD IN MEDIÆVAL LITERATURE.

When Homer described the pretty fright of Astyanax in his nurse's arms, amid the parting of Hector and Andromache; when Vergil made Damon recall the day when, as a little boy just able to reach up to the branches, he saw his mother and the child who was to be his fate gathering apples—the hyacinths of Theocritus were daintier—they struck two chords of feeling, one charming, the other deeper and richer, which have started vibrations whenever they have met a sympathetic reader ever since. Because we are susceptible to the poetry of childhood we are pleased to find that these ancient poets also cared for it. It adds a personal touch to our feeling for them. It gives us a thrill of the immortality of heart and its simplest, purest sentiment. There may be an element of the fictitious in our feeling about childhood. Heaven may not be about our infancy, those "sweet early days" may not have been "as long as twenty days are now"; and they may not have been the types of innocence, simplicity, the loveliness of the race taken at first hand from nature, which we fancy them. But there is something beyond a fallacy in this sentiment; it is in our purer and more refined moods that we are sensitive to it. Like a whiff of spring smoke, or woodsy odors, a reminder of our early life will sometimes throw us into a revery which is more than recollection. No one can write well about children without sensibility to youthful emotion and some love for family life. Whoever looks back with genial wistfulness upon his own early days, and enjoys renewing them in the playthings of his fancy, can hardly be without a vein of quiet refinement. When an age listens with pleasure to such sketches, it is not barren of the homely affections, nor uniformly given over to restless and unlawful passions. As one wanders through the poetry of the middle ages, one observes the frequency with which it mentions children.

These passages, judged absolutely, may not be remarkable for insight or tenderness, but in those days all emotional subjects were treated crudely. Yet they are often interesting for themselves, and they show a fact which many seem to question that the sentiments of simple family life were felt by poets and people. So much has been written by critics upon the worse side of the society of chivalry, that it is well to recognize this other aspect of its affections. The public has frequently been assured that those days knew nothing of true family sentiment. How much truth there is in the statement that fashionable love disregarded marriage, has been shown in a preceding essay. But on *a priori* grounds we should disbelieve that general society was permeated by artificial gallantry. Even were the testimony of lyrical lovers uniform, we must recollect how conventional all their love-poetry was; most poets composed on formal lines impersonally, in spite of their pronouns. One of the troubadours, indeed, denied that this was possible when the husband of his theme challenged him, in the lonely place where he was hunting, by his liege truth to tell him whether he had a lady love. "Sire," he replied, "how could I sing unless I loved?" But in most poems there was more business, or ambitious art, than nature. A large number of these poets impress us as having just as little emotional veracity in writing as had Cowley in *The Mistress*. Moreover, even if a school of poetry, not conventionalized, should treat romantic and sensational sentiment to the exclusion of domestic, it would prove nothing. What if cynical critics some centuries hence should give Mr. Coventry Patmore a place in their encyclopedias, simply on the ground that he was an exception to the nineteenth-century belief that love ended at the bridal altar? Possibly by that time love, poetry, and fiction may deal mainly with domestic emotions after marriage, and then our own romances will very likely appear strange.

From one point of view those centuries were too akin to undeveloped life to be prepared to represent it. Europe seven hundred years ago seems like a vast nursery abandoned by its governess. The people are like children of various ages and sizes, degrees of education, and innate sense of right and wrong. Children are impulsive, passionate, selfish, brutally inconsiderate; they are sometimes religious too. We find apparently sporadic susceptibility to isolation and prayer. They cry at trifles, and while their cheeks are still wet, they are smiling. Bright and simple things please them; they are fickle and impatient; they love lively music; when they are tired playing, nothing pleases them like a story—they listen intently, credulously. When spring comes they can no more help running and dancing over the grass, than sunbeams on a brook. The gentler sit in the meadow making posies, while the rougher are setting traps, and racing, and fighting: but sometimes the rough boys will come and play in the meadow, and be pleasant to the girls. All these traits of children apply to the mediæval character, their barbarisms, their ethical inconsistencies, their delight in stories (no age has ever cared more for story telling), their love of play, their passion for spring, and the rest.

Undoubtedly the popular impression gives the period too little joyousness. Mercurial childhood has capacity for sudden pleasures even when life goes ill, and life frequently went very well even then. But the mystery and grace of motherhood and dawning life are likely to appeal to a calmer and more retrospective age. The seriousness that takes pleasure in contemplating childhood is more serene and pensive than the usual moods of an era undeveloped emotionally. So it would not be a matter for surprise if the literary remains of those days had left us mainly incidental references to children.

Of such plain facts we have many, such as, for instance, that the little ones were entertained with pet dogs, birds, and squirrels (apparently never with cats), mice harnessed to a toy wagon, clay or wooden images of animals, and tiny vessels after kitchen models, toy men, women, and children, tops, and marbles; that they played blind man's buff, and many games attended with songs. As early as the interesting Latin poem called *Waltharius et Hiltgunde*, which at least in a popular version Walther von der Vogelweide liked, we find the hero appealing to Hagen, by the memory of the boyish games with which they had whiled away their childhood, and over which they never had quarrelled.

We obtain considerable information about customs of education also; such as the attention paid to languages (a girl in a French romance is said to have understood fourteen tongues), and Isolde knew French and Latin as well as Irish. Boys were sent off on their travels early, going especially to Paris. Weinhold's quotation from Hugo von Trimberg illustrates the dangers that beset the pursuit of culture even then: "Many boys go to Paris; they learn little and spend much. But yet no doubt they see Paris."

When Sir Philip Sidney derided the contemporary drama's habit of carrying a play through a large part of the hero's lifetime, instead of restricting the action to a developed episode, he made a poor criticism, out of tune, as are other parts of his criticism, with the genius of Elizabethan poetry. But the passage is interesting as a reminder of the relation to that great literature of the romances which runs back through the middle ages to the later Greek writings. Such narrations as the *Daphnis and Chloe*, and the *Aethiopica*, introduce their central characters while they are still children, and whether through transmitted influence or independently, the same course is pursued by the most important romance poems of mediæval France and Germany. To this practice we owe pleasant domestic scenes of many a hero's early life, and sometimes, indeed, a narration of early joys and sorrows of his parents' love. The *Tristan* of Gottfried von Strassburg, for example, begins well before the birth of its subject, with noteworthy romantic episodes. This brilliant poem's account of the early years of chivalry's typical fine gentleman illustrates the admiration paid to intellectual training at a time when polite society in general was not well educated. Tristan spent his first seven years under the care of his foster-mother, learning various lessons of good behavior; after that Rual li Foitenant provided a master, and sent him off to acquire foreign languages in their own lands, and "book-learning" as well. The luxurious temper of his chronicler stops for a long sigh at the hardship of such training, through the years when joyousness is at its best. So it is, he exclaims in his studied style, with many youth; when life is in its first bloom and freedom, away they are constrained to go from its free blossom. For seven years this young prince was constantly kept busy with the exercises of arms and horsemanship, in addition to his formal studies; he also learned hunting, and all courtly arts, especially music. Then he was called home to be prepared for his political career. The education of children was assisted by not a few treatises on manners and morals, such as *Babees Books*, as the old English called them. They are usually manuals of etiquette, mediæval prototypes of such modern works as *Don't*. Chaucer's Prioress had evidently studied the sections on table proprieties, and her gentility, which was so tender-hearted, might well have been developed under the admonishments of the ethical passages which often accompanied them. For a tender age many of these precepts were depressing. One of the gravest and most mature of these works is called *Der Winsbeke*, with a sequel, *Die Winsbekin*, for girls, the advice of a twelfth-century Solomon, which moralizes certainly as well as most of its analogues. This stanza, for instance, shows a homely dignity:

That bright candle mark, my son,While it burns, it wastes away;So from thee thy life doth run,(I say true) from day to day.In thy memory let this dwell,And life here so rule, that thenWith thy soul it may be well.What though wealth exalt thy name?Only this shall follow thee—A linen cloth to hide thy shame.

These gnomic writings, running into a developed didacticism, are illustrated by the song of Walther von der Vogelweide on the restraint of eye, ear, and tongue. Whether this poet was the teacher of the young King Henry, as some have thought, or gained his experience in humbler ways, he evidently knew the trials of the pedagogue. "Oh, you self-willed boy," he cries, "too small to be put to work in the field and too big to whip, have your own way and go to sleep." As for flogging, this prince of the minnesingers took the side of the Matthew Feildes against the Boyers: "No one can switch a child into education; to those whom you can bring up well, a word is as good as a blow." Apropos of the teacher's view, we also find the pupil's feeling for his teacher recorded in that little poem of the English school-boy, who was late in the morning, and explained to the master that his mother told him to stop and milk the ducks. The boy recounts the details of what follows, and afterwards, instead of taking up his interrupted studies, he words out a day-dream in which the master is turned into a hare, his books into hounds, and the boy goes hunting.

There is a grain of humor, too, at least for the modern reader, in a much more sentimental child-play of the minnesinger Hadlaub. Though he mainly echoes the love singers who wrote a hundred years before him, one of the first songs in the collection of his poems raises a hope of something more than the ordinary, though this only leads us on to disappointment through the rest of his fifty-odd pieces. There is something very natural about this picture of the lover catching sight of his disdainful fair one playing with a little child. "She reached out her arms and caught it close to her, she took its face between her white hands, and pressed it to her lips and mouth and lovely cheek; ah, how deliciously she kissed it!" What did the child do? "Just what I should have done; threw its arms around her, and was so happy." When she let the little one go, the lover went after it and kissed it just where her lips had been, "and how that went to my heart!" Poor fellow! "I serve her since we both were children," and this is the nearest apparently that he ever came to the seals of love.

But instead of delaying over estrays, pleasant scraps like those left us by Heinrich von Morungen, for instance, one of the few minnesingers for whom one really cares, we may pass on to three or four more detailed examples from the thirteenth century, of household love and sympathy with the poetry of childhood. But first I will translate a simple sesame for opening again the early gates. The poet is known as the Wild Alexander, but his mood was gentle and gracious when this revery of his boyhood came upon him:

There we children used to play,Thro' the meadows and away,Looking 'mid the grassy mazeFor the violets; those daysLong agoSaw them grow;Now one sees the cattle graze.

I remember as we faredThro' the blossoms, we comparedWhich the prettiest might be:We were little things, you see.On the groundWreaths we bound;—So it goes, our youth and we.

Over stick and stone we wentTill the sunny day was spent;Hunting strawberries each skirrsFrom the beeches to the firs,Till—Hello,Children! GoHome, they cry—the foresters.

So he goes on to tell how their childhood took as a pleasure the hurts and stings that they received as they hunted for strawberries, and to recall the warnings against snakes that the herdsman sometimes shouted through the branches. Apart from its graceful manner, and the breezy freshness of its universal childhood, the poem's specific touches are unusual. "From the beeches to the firs," for instance, does not sound mediæval aside from one's surprise that a German should have omitted the linden. We need not be as old as was Lamb in 1820, to look back with a touch of desire on the child, that other me, there in the background. Perhaps there is the glamour of sentiment about that familiar association of childhood with purity and moral grace. Yet the feeling appeals to us as true beyond mere beauty, and many may read with responsiveness these lines, hitherto unprinted, by one on whose lips, just parted for their song, silence laid her finger:

"Could I answer love like thine,All earth to me were heaven anew;But were thy heart, dear child, as mine,What place for love between us two?Bright things for tired eyes vainly shine:A grief the pure heaven's simple blue.Alas, for lips past joy of wine,That find no blessing in God's dew!From dawning summits crystallineThou lookest down; thou makest signToward this bleak vale I wander through.I cannot answer; that pure shrineOf childhood, though my love be true,Is hidden from my dim confine:I must not hope for clearer view.The sky, the earth, the wrinkled brineWould wear to me a fresher hue,And all once more be half-divine,Could I answer love like thine."

The spiritual subtlety of such a mood certainly is beyond the mediæval poets, yet we find pleasant proofs of sensibility to the tender, unselfish nature of a loving child. Nowhere in such detail, perhaps, as in the most familiar of Middle High German poems, the *Poor Henry*, of Hartmann von Aue. The story is known in Longfellow's *Golden Legend*. This is not the place to discuss that poem, which contains some charming passages. The poet's treatment may be far from satisfactory, yet when he calls his original the most beautiful of mediæval legends, he certainly shows a more satisfactory side of extreme estimate than does Goethe, in his curious fling at the poem (which we may notice he read in a modernized form). He says it gave him a "physico-æsthetic pain," and adds that the notion of a fine girl sacrificing herself for a leper, affected him so that he felt himself poisoned by the book. This judgment was pronounced in Goethe's later life, and is consistent with his habitual want of sympathy with mediæval romantic literature. It shows, moreover, a lack of historical adjustment, for the dreadful disease was so common in the twelfth century that its repulsiveness was blurred for Hartmann; yet he mentions it with the greatest reserve, though a description of its appearance could hardly be more painful than the famous conclusion of the *De Rerum Natura*. We are reminded of Goethe's visit to Assisi, interesting to him only as the situation of some remains of classical architecture.[10]

Hartmann von Aue ranks below his two great companions in German narrative poetry, for he is more of a translator than either Gottfried or Wolfram. His distinction is in his style; he has a very agreeable way of telling a story, and there is a quiet charm about his diction. "How clear and pure his crystal words are and always must be," is Gottfried's tribute. We come to feel a personal liking for him, through his unaffected interest in his characters, his unassuming ways and the tact by which he lightens or deepens his accentuation. We feel that he was a gentleman, and we do not wonder at the kind regard in which all his fellow poets held him. We like his refined moral seriousness and that calm temperament of which he speaks in *Gregorius*. The original for the *Arme Heinrich* is lost, but though his introduction claims for himself no merit beyond a careful selection out of the many books that he takes pains to tell us he was learned enough to read for himself, we are probably justified in feeling that he took his heart into partnership when he made the version, receiving from it touches that he did not find in the earlier treatment. To appreciate the poem we have to put ourselves into harmony with the wonder-loving, credulous, and mystically religious world of seven hundred years ago. Hartmann's simple earnestness and unobtrusive tenderness and piety constitute an ideal manner for the legend, and that ease of his soul which he hoped would come through the prayers of those who read the poem after his death, is perhaps equally well secured if he knows how some of his verses touch the sophisticated sense of to-day. He said that he was actuated in writing by the desire to soften hard hours in a way that would be to the honor of God, and by which he might make himself dear to others. He has succeeded. It is to the honor of God, and it wins the affection of others, when a poet leads his readers to a little well of pure unselfish love, hedged about by a child's religious faith.

The hero of the legend is a gentleman of position and feudal possessions, whose free and generous career is cut short by an incurable leprosy. It is in vain that he consults masters at Montpelier and Salerno, the famous seats of medicine; and the honor and affection in which a genial life had established him among his friends cannot save him from becoming a social outcast. He disposes of his wealth between the poor and the church, and retires to a fief whose tenant is willing to receive his suzerain as a guest. Here, on a little estate, away from all contact with the world, the gay lord resigns himself to the companionship of the farmer and his wife, whose gratitude for his kindness in the past distinguishes them among the multitude to whom his amiable disposition had made him a benefactor and friend. There were children in the family, the eldest a girl eight years old, when Henry came. It was because their hearts were loyal that her parents were kind, but she kept close by him because she loved to be there. She was always to be found at his feet, and his affectionate nature liked her companionship. He bought her a hand mirror, a riband for her hair, a belt and finger ring, and whatever children care for. These gifts attached her to him, yet the main secret of her love was the sweet spirit that God had given her. After three years, as the family were sitting together one day with their high-born guest, the farmer asked him why it was that he had given himself up so hopelessly to his disease, and Henry laid aside his reserve, and told for the first time about his visit to the great physician at Salerno. The only remedy was an impossible one. He might indeed be healed, but not unless a virgin made a voluntary offering of her life. Alas, God was his only physician.

The little girl, who was so inseparable a companion that he jestingly called her his bride, listened as she was holding her sick lord's feet in her lap. She could not get it out of her head (the old German idiom is better, "out of her heart") the rest of the day, and when at night she lay in her usual place at her father's and mother's feet, she felt so sorry for her dear lord that she cried, and the warm tears fell on her parents' feet, and woke them. When they asked her what was the matter, she said that she thought they ought to be sorry, too; for what would happen to them all if their lord should die? Some one else would own the farm, and no one could ever be as kind to them as he had been. They told her that was all true, but it could do no good to lament. "Dear child, do not grieve. We feel as badly as you do, but alas, we cannot help him." So they hushed her, but all the night and the next day she continued to be unhappy, and whatever else she was doing, she kept thinking of this. When she went to bed, she cried again, till finally she resolved to herself that if she lived till morning she would surely give her life for her lord. Straightway from that thought, she became lighthearted and happy, and felt free of all her cares, until it occurred to her that perhaps Henry and her parents would not permit her to make the sacrifice; whereupon the poor little girl burst out crying again, and wakened her parents, as she had done the night before. It was only with difficulty that they drew from her this simple speech: "My lord might get well in the way that he told us, and if you will only let me, I am what he needs for being cured. I am a maid, and rather than see him pass away, I will die for him." A long dialogue follows, in which the parents remonstrate with the daughter, who replies in a strain of spiritual elation. She appeals not only to her parents' worldly dependence on their master's goodness, but also to their desire for her own highest welfare. How much better for her to pass to eternal life in unstained childhood, only anticipating the death that must come some time, no less unwelcome late than soon. Her parents ceased to remonstrate, for they felt that the Holy Ghost was speaking through her, as they listened to the visionary cry. Instead of taking, two or three years hence, some neighbor for her husband, she will choose

> "the Franklin, who is wooing me to a home where the plough runs easily, where there is all abundance, where horses and cattle never are lost, where no wailing children suffer, where it is neither too warm nor too cold, where the old will grow young, where is nor frost nor hunger, no kind of pain, but all joy without toil; thither will I haste me, and forsake a farm whose tillage, fire, hail, and flood destroy, so that one half-day ruins the labor of a year.

Then let me go to our Lord Jesus Christ, whose grace is sure, and who loves me, poor as I am, like a queen."

Unlike our modern analysts of character, Hartmann does not stop to comment on the art of his delineation, and it is possible to miss the tact with which he keeps his heroine's renunciation consistent with a child's nature. Hartmann is not treating this character inartistically, as a mere instrument for religious culture. Earnest speech of a thoughtful parish priest; or phrases caught from the conversation of her lord touched by his sorrows, with the age's feeling *de contemptu mundi*, might have supplied her with some sentiments that seem beyond a child's invention, and children's emotions are sometimes precocious, especially in what seems a morbid religious development.

Those are the years of faith, credulous belief that burns with the white light of knowledge; a child's faith is a man's superstition. The peasant maid's imagination sees heaven and salvation a fact so infinitely desirable, that all dread of death was eliminated from the path of her love. The joyousness of her sacrifice, too, instead of being a romantic exaggeration, is far truer to life than a willingness touched with pain and hesitation could have been. In a noble dread, austerely controlled, lies Calvary's dignity and pathos. But her gratitude and impetuous love for what seems to her simple mind a superior and infinitely deserving object, reached that finest pitch of selfishness, where self-sacrifice becomes the demand of impulsive egotism. To an enthusiastic temperament love's passionate altruism may be consummate self-will. As the little maid came away from her deliverance, though she was happy in her lord's restoration, she was less happy than as she went.

For she did not have to die. In the tyranny of undeniable love, she broke down the opposition of her parents, and although Henry indeed hesitated, she pleaded so anxiously and drew such an eloquent sketch of the advantage and gladness death would be to her, and the value of his life compared with hers, that at last, genial and affectionate as he was, the temptation to live by the sacrifice of a mere child's life (and the feudal sense of possession ought not to be overlooked) was too strong to be resisted. Compare the scene with the one in *Philaster*, where Bellario wishes to offer herself for the man whom she loves with a hopeless earthly sentiment:

"'Tis not a life,'Tis but a piece of childhood thrown away."

For her, continuance of life is only "a game that must be lost." But for the nameless German girl there is no pathos in living, beyond the thought of her master's death, and her sentiment was as childlike as when it began, while she was only eight years old. Her love is a flame that burns impatiently away from the taper that feeds it; for her generous passion is after all a beautiful devoted wilfulness. When her parents wept to lose her, and her lord wept at his own weak hesitation, she wept above them all and her tears won the day. She rode with Henry to Salerno, and was unhappy only because the journey was so long. The great physician took her hand, and led her alone into a barred and bolted room. Then he tried to frighten her and induce her to retract her consent, but she only laughed until she became afraid that he would not do his part, whereupon she broke out into an indignant scorn for his unmanly weakness. When he bade her undress, she did so without a blush; he bound her to his table, and took up his knife. He wished to render death easy (so he told himself), and taking a whetstone to make the knife sharper, he slowly whetted it—only as a pretext for delaying. The gentleman outside found himself restless. He listened, then he tried to look in and at last through a crevice in the wall he saw that "little bride" who had been his main companion and comfort during those three wretched years. By a fine touch of nature, the poet makes the sight of her perfect loveliness as she lay waiting for her celestial bridal, the force that broke the selfish charm which had enchained his manliness. He beat on the door, he called, and when no response came, he burst his way in. "The child is too lovely to die. For myself, God's will be done."

It was now that her trial came, as she wailed and beat wildly at her body, to force on him the life he was unwilling to take. She talked bitterly and peevishly, as if she had been cheated of heaven through his cruelty. But it was in vain, he dressed her again in the rich garments which he had procured for the sacrificial journey, and they set out on their return to their distant home, the sobbing girl and the leper. But as they rode along, the divine might that seemed so near to mediæval faith was their companion, and touching the incurable disease, fulfilled love's miracle. Henry took their daughter back to the peasants, and gave her rich gifts, while he presented them with the land which they had farmed, and all its serfs and chattels. Then he went back to his estates, and to the welcome that the world was waiting to give him. By and by, when his people insisted that he should marry, he called an old-time conference about whom he should choose. There were numerous suggestions, but the advisers did not agree. He listened, and then telling them that unless they would approve his own choice, he should never marry, he stepped to the side of "the dear little wife" who had loved him as a leper.

The romance of *Fleur et Blanchefleur*, which goes back, though not in its present form, to the twelfth century, enjoyed such popularity that it was translated into almost every European tongue. Indeed, in some languages it is found in more than one version. The story tells of a Saracen prince, whose royal father interrupts the smooth course of his true love for a

Christian girl. She was the daughter of a captive lady in the palace of the Queen, and the royal boy and the bond girl had been born on the same day. From his birth, the mother of Blanchefleur became Fleur's nurse; the pagan law required that he must be suckled by a heathen, but in all other ways the infants were treated like twins. They slept in one cradle, and when they could eat and drink they were given the same food. Thus they grew up together, until they were five years old, when the King, seeing his child as fine and promising a boy as could be found in any land, decided that it was time for him to begin his education. He selected a master, but Fleur, when he was bidden to study, burst into tears and cried, "Sire, what will Blanchefleur do? Who will teach her? I never can learn without her." The King answered that since he loved her so, Blanchefleur should go with him to school.

> "So they went and came together, and the joy of their love was still uninterrupted. It was a wonder to see how each of the two studied for each; neither learned anything without straightway telling the other. At nature's earliest, all their concern was love; they were quick in learning and well they remembered. Pagan books that spake of love they read together with delight; these hastened them along in the understanding and joy of love. On their way home from school, they would put their arms about each other, and kiss. In the King's garden, bright with all plants and flowers of various hues, they went to play every morning, and to eat their dinner; and after they had eaten, they listened to the birds singing in the trees above them, and then they went their way back to school, and a happy walk they found it. When they were again at school they took their ivory tablets, and you might have seen them writing letters and verses of love, in the wax. Deftly with their gold and silver styles they made letters and greeting of love, of the songs of birds and of flowers. This was all they cared for. In five years and fifteen days, they both had learned to write neatly on parchment, and to talk in Latin so well that no one could understand."

When we follow the poem along, we find in the different versions many familiar romance expedients, conventional incidents of the pathetic, exciting, and marvellous, but the charm is in the unwavering love of these twins, who from the hour of birth breathed together, even in their sleep, yet no kin to each other, and blending brotherhood and sisterhood with the other love of man and woman in perfection, since for neither they knew the beginning. In this way the mediæval romance is even more ideal than

Beaumont's *Triumph of Love*, where Gerard and Violante passed from the sentiment of childhood "as innocently as the first lovers ere they fell."

"Gerard's and my affection began," the heroine tells Ferdinand,

"In infancy: my uncle brought him oftIn long clothes hither; you were such another.The little boy would kiss me, being a child,And say he loved me: give me all his toys,Bracelets, rings, sweetmeats, all his rosy smiles;I then would stand and stare upon his eyes,Play with his locks, and swear I loved him too.For sure, methought he was a little Love,He wooed so prettily in innocenceThat then he warmed my fancy; for I feltA glimmering beam of love kindle my bloodBoth which time since hath made a flame and flood."

In the early stages of Fleur's love-trials his parents attempted to persuade him that Blanchefleur was dead, and to give confirmation to their assertions they caused a superb tomb to be constructed, in a style that is of considerable interest in the study of literary origins from its obviously Oriental tone. Without delaying for its rich and curious Eastern details, we may yet notice the sentiment in the figures of the boy and girl that were placed upon it. "Never were seen images of fairer children, or more like to the lovers. The image of Blanchefleur holds a flower before Fleur, before her lover holds the fair one a rose of fine bright gold; and before her, Fleur holds a blanched golden fleur-de-lis. Close by each other they sit, a sweet look on their faces." A mechanical device is so contrived that when the wind blew and touched the children they embraced and kissed, and by necromancy they spoke to each other as in their childhood, and thus said Fleur to Blanchefleur: "Kiss me, sweet," and kissing him, she replied: "I love you more than all the world."

The story of Fleur and Blanchefleur was so popular that they became identified with the characters of another romance, and were sung of as the parents of Berte-as-graus-pies, the heroine of an attractive legend, and the mythical mother of Charlemagne. In the poem that relates her misfortunes after she has been sent from Hungary to France as the wife of Pepin, we find a suggestion of the depth of sentiment that was always associated with her legendary parents. She has been in France almost nine years without their having heard from her, and Blanchefleur determines to undertake a journey to see her child again before she dies. The King, without opposing her desire, expresses a half remonstrance that we may add to the other proofs in mediæval poetry, that true love in our modern sense was familiar throughout those eras: "Oh, my lady, how shall we be able to live so long without each other?" Let us believe that in the Utopia where these lovers who loved from their birth resided, they found, after their own sharp trials and the trials of their daughter were safely over, a serene old age, out of which they passed unconsciously some night, sleeping themselves away in each other's arms.

This love between boy and girl was attractive to the old narrative poets. The greatest of them all touched the soul of young romance when he said of Sigune and Schionatulander, "Alas, they are still too young for such pain, yet 'tis the love of youth which lasts." Wolfram gives us pretty touches of childhood as far back as the nursery; like that of a mother and her ladies playing over the new-born baby, or of children learning to stand by taking hold of chairs, and creeping over the floor to reach them, or of Sigune's care to take her box of dolls with her when she went away. "Whoever saw this little girl thought her a glimpse of May among the dewy flowers." As she grew older, too, he describes her, assuming the airs of a young lady. "When her breasts were rounding and her light wavy hair began to turn dark, she grew more proud and dignified, though always keeping her womanlike sweetness." The story of her love with Schionatulander has delightful stanzas; their long love-pleading dialogue is much truer than most of the minnesingers' work in its restraint and in the girl's coy sweetness. She is an earlier Dorigen as she watches for the beloved who does not come, wasting many an evening at the window gazing over the fields, or climbing to the housetop to look. But what distinguishes the author of the *Titurel* above his fellow-poets is his sentiment for something more than romance. Children are dear to him, and the wife is dearer. His idea of love consists no more in Dante's platonic mysticism than in passion and inconstancy. Without transcendentalism its dominant tone is spiritual. Compare an earlier lover's cry in the loveliest of French romances: "What is there in heaven for me? I will never go there without Nicolette, my sweet darling, whom I love so much. It is to hell that fine gentlemen go and pretty, well-bred ladies who love." Compare that Parisian type of feeling with this of Wolfram: "Love between man and woman has its house on earth, and its pure guidance leads us to God and heaven. This love is everywhere save in hell!" To such a poet we naturally turn for the deepest mediæval note in the treatment of childhood, and we do not listen in vain.

"What a difference there is between women," Wolfram exclaims. It seems to him the way of modern womanhood to be disloyal, worldly, selfish, like men: but in the days of which he writes in his chief poem there was a lady Herzeloide, to whom after her husband's death in the wars, the sun was a cloud, the world's joy lost, night and day alike, who for heavenly riches chose earthly poverty, and leaving her estates went with her retainers far into the unreclaimed forest to bring up her infant safe from the strife and wiles of men. This only heritage of her lost lord was the boy Parzival. She trusted that by hiding him away from all knowledge of the world, she might always keep him her own. She exacted an oath from her servants that they would never let him hear of knights and knighthood, and while they cleared farming land in the heart of the woods, she cared for the child. It was a desolate place, but she was not looking for meadows and flowers; she gave no thought to wreaths, whether red or yellow.[11]

The child grew into boyhood, and was indulged in making bows and arrows. As he played in the woods, he shot some of the birds. But after he saw them dead, he remembered how they had sung, and he cried. Every morning he went to a stream to bathe. There was nothing to trouble him, except the singing of the birds over his head: but that was so sweet that his breast grew strained with feeling; and he ran to his mother in tears. She asked what ailed him, but "like children even now it may be," he could not tell her. But she kept the riddle in her heart, and one day she found him gazing up at the trees listening to the birds, and she saw how his breast heaved as they sang. It seemed to her that she hated them, she did not know why. She wanted to stop their singing, and bade her farm hands snare and kill them. But the birds were too quick; most of them remained and kept on singing. The boy asked his mother what harm the birds did, and if the war upon them might not cease. She kissed his lips:

> "Why am I opposing highest God? Shall the birds lose their happiness because of me?"

> "Nay, mother, what is God?"

> "My son, He is brighter than the day; He took upon himself the likeness of man. When trouble comes upon thee, pray to him: his faithfulness upholds the world. The Devil is darkness; turn thy thoughts from him, and from unbelief."

This passage is Wolfram's invention; the brilliant Gallic poet whose romance he followed could not have contrived it. This sympathy with nature belongs to our later era; it seems less strange to meet it in Keats, when the boy Apollo wanders out alone in the morning twilight:

"The nightingale had ceased, and a few starsWere lingering in the heavens, while the thrushBegan calm-throated. Throughout all the isleThere was no covert, no retired caveUnhaunted by the murmurous noise of waves.Though scarcely heard in many a green recess,He listened and he wept, and his bright tearsWent trickling down the golden bow he held."

One recalls nothing in the two centuries which Wolfram touches that equals this picture of the mother watching her child's baptism with the sad and precious gift of soul, as he stands gazing upward in his forest trance, or

- 93 -

listening to his dawning perplexities, or teaching him his first religious lesson, or jealous of the birds, because his dreamy love for them dimly warned her of a mysterious growing soul that would not remain within her simple call. Those lines in the *Princess* of the faith in womankind and the trust in all things high, that come easy to the son of a good mother, certainly are appropriate to Parzival, whose faith held true and simple through his whole career as the foremost knight of chivalric legend, living for a spiritual ideal, unseduced by beauty and the ways of courts from loyalty to his first wedlock:

"True to the kindred points of heaven and home."

The description of Parzival's meeting with the knights, his mistaking them in their bright armor for angels, and his eagerness to make his way to Arthur's court are narrated by Chrestien with his own excellent vivacity, and here Wolfram only follows.

The Welsh version of the story in the *Mabinogi* of Peredur, though disappointing, contains a naïve sketch of the boy's rustic attempt to imitate the knight's trappings. But for the full tenderness of his mother's parting as he goes out from home to the fierce world we must turn again to the German.[12]

She kisses him, and as he rides away "runs a few steps after him" till he has galloped out of sight and then she closes forever the eyes whose light of motherhood shone like a star above the sea, over those tumultuous years.

All through these centuries there are poems to the Virgin, especially in Latin, which manifest similar sensibility to infancy and motherhood. One of the most pleasing belongs to England, and is written in the commixture of Latin and the modern tongue, which occasionally produces quaintly pretty effects. The glorified Christ summons his mother, by the memory of their kisses when she calmed him in sweet song, to come and be crowned. "Pulcra ut luna"—lovely as moonlight—"veni coronaberis."

But perhaps the most delicate of all such sketches comes from an unexpected source. A young lawyer in the town of Todi, whose early life had combined pleasure with sufficient study to gain the doctorate, was turned aside from a prosperous public career by the tragical loss of his bride. Matthew Arnold has given a symbolism to the story of her death in the sonnet beginning:

"That son of Italy who tried to blow'Ere Dante came, the trump of sacred song."

The sorrow struck deep, even to the point of partial mania; the gay young man forsook the world and devoted years to seclusion and religious culture. Later in 1278, he entered the order of the Minorites, and ranks as one of their delirious enthusiasts, a mystic poet, a reckless satirist of evils in high places. His fanatic asceticism made him glory in bodily torments and the world's scorn. The nickname, Jacopone, he carried proudly, and even the harshness of Boniface VIII. could not quell his zest for martyrdom. We should scarcely look to him for sympathy with the sweet gaieties of the nursery, yet this little sketch of the Virgin's life with Christ, the child, came from the same hand that wrote the sorrows of the *Stabat Mater*.

Ah sweet, how sweet, the love within thy heart,When on thy breast the nursing infant lay:What gentle actions, sweetly loving play,Thine, with thy holy child apart.When for a little while he sometimes slept,Thou eager to awake thy paradise,Soft, soft, so that he could not hear thee, crept,And laidest thy lips close to his eyes,Then, with the smile maternal calling, "Nay,'Twere naughty to sleep longer, wake, I say!"

The almost incoherent repetition of the word "Love," in one of his poems, is suggestive of the man; despair for human love led to his half-crazed absorption in the divine. Very sweetly sounds this sacred meditation's echo of his recollection of the nights of his own childhood, of which he has told, when his mother, as she waked, would make a light and come and lean over his bed, till sometimes his eyes would open to see her watching him there. His father did not spare the rod for the careless boy, nor in later years did the father of his soul; but the divine motherhood of memory and of present faith bent with yearning eyes, we may be sure, over his anxious sleep in prison or in the ascetic cell.

But it was only the greatest of all these poets who could leave us the lovely image of the new-born soul that comes forth in its simplicity from the hand that loves it before its birth, playing like a young girl who weeps and smiles. Yet Dante's principal sensation about childhood is its helplessness, and the mother's eyes, which throw its aureole about infancy, do not seem to have held their tenderest meaning for him. He would never have gone beyond the original ten lines of

"She was a phantom of delight."

But he gives beauty to the child's frightened eyes when they meet its mother's, and certainly the vision, whether real or imagined, toward the close of the *Vita Nuova* will please forever. This straying love is recalled to its old faithfulness by "the strong imagination" of a little figure that is habited in red, just as it had appeared to him when, perhaps in Folco's Florentine garden, the boy not quite nine fell in love with the girl of eight.

Perhaps Boccaccio's story of the falcon is too familiar to quote, though it illustrates domestic love too well to be unmentioned. One hardly can choose the best of its touches—the bright account of the boy running over the fields with his mother's old-time lover, as he hawked, always eying with a boy's eagerness for ownership the famous falcon, the only remnant of Frederick's gay and wealthy life, which he had lost for the unsuccessful love; or the picture of the mother again and again begging the child, as he lay ill, to tell her something which he desired, so that she might obtain it for him; until his feverish imagination persuaded him that to have the wonderful falcon would make him well again; or our thought of the impoverished gentleman, whose devotion had lasted under the years of exile on his little farm, his hope departed, who when suddenly visited by his widowed love, and finding nothing in the larder, nor money, nor even anything valuable enough for a pledge to secure some entertainment for her, desperately wrung the neck of his precious bird; or the delicate hesitation and awkwardness of the lady when she came to explain her errand, and the struggle, before love for her child bent both pride and pity; or the lover's broken heart when he found that his excess of devotion had cost him his only opportunity of pleasing her. The whole may be read in a little play of Tennyson's later years, or among the *Tales of a Wayside Inn*; but it is much better to read it in the narrative of the Certaldesian. Tuscany has sent us down no tenderer story.

A MEDIÆVAL WOMAN.[13]

When Heloise was born, just after the twelfth century opened, Abelard, through whom she was to experience the deepest ecstacies and the most poignant distress, and by whose union with her life she was to become the most famous mediæval woman, was a young man of twenty-two. He came of a rather high-bred family in Brittany; his father, though an active soldier, was interested in letters and took pains to have his children instructed in the ornaments as well as the defence of life. This eldest son, so attracted by his early lessons that he determined to sacrifice his rights of primogeniture, and to renounce the distinction of a knightly career for the life of study, while yet a youth started out as a student-tramp, one of a multitude who wandered from town to town to hear lectures on the seven topics that made up the educational curriculum of the age. Through this entire epoch, for generation after generation, this practice of student vagrancy continued: now the intellectual centre was England, now France, now Germany; sometimes two or three teachers would draw crowds to the exclusion of all other schools, sometimes the numbers would divide up among scores of masters. Poor, rich, coarse, refined, hard-working, indolent, quick-witted, stupid, scholars, impostors,—these student crowds were an extraordinary medley. To realize the irregularity and the strangeness of their lives we have to read such a story as Freytag quotes[14] from Thomas Platter, a wandering scholar of the fifteenth century. Such German students were perhaps of a lower grade than the young men who travelled through France three hundred years before, and the standard of scholarship may have been inferior, but their general experiences must have been similar, and most of Abelard's companions no doubt were mentally crude, arrogant, superstitious; many dissipated and even brutal. Yet some were touched by the love of truth, and had vigorous minds, well trained by application. The majority of these better men were of course hedged in by the palisades of Catholic tradition, and sought knowledge from the past, rather than from independent present thought: but there were some whose ideas were bolder, and who kept proposing questions which their teachers did not answer.

The deferential attention with which Roscellinus and William of Champeaux were listened to, was broken in upon when the handsome youth Abelard appeared at the schools of these leaders of European thought. The strength of each was in dialectics, the topic which then held intellectual interest to the practical disregard of almost every other subject except the theology into which it played, and they took opposite sides on the absorbing problem of general terms. In the school of each, Abelard rose as a disputant; he challenged his teacher to argue with him as an equal until he triumphed in turn over the extreme Nominalist and the extreme Realist. Then he set up schools of his own, which he moved from place to place, as the intolerant hostility of his vanquished chiefs and their upholders required. His reputation steadily rose, and he drew the largest and most enthusiastic following, for the keenest young thought of the generation recognized in him its natural leader.

All independence and liberality of mind must be estimated relatively to the age concerned. From our outlook Abelard seems a narrow and constrained thinker, but to the churchman of the opening of the twelfth century he was a rationalist, a daring explorer into the sacred mysteries that must be accepted by the sealed eye of Faith. How absurd, he exclaims, to teach what you cannot give reasons for believing. So he tried to make belief a matter for intellectual comprehension; he argued where others asserted, and made bold to modify current opinions which his ingenuity, often childishly simple, could not explain. He had a noble grasp upon some conceptions far beyond the reach of his antagonists. He independently developed the ethical doctrine that the value of conduct is in motive, not in act; he taught that the main worth of the incarnation was to present the model of a perfect life; that the man Christ Jesus was not a member of the Trinity; that the love of God is as freely bestowed on sinner as on saint; that God could not prevent evil, or he would have done so. For the sufferings that he endured in teaching his pupils to use not credulity but unflinching independent thought in their reflections even on theology, he deserves our grateful admiration.

When Abelard was thirty-eight years old he was at the height of his reputation. Technical and abstruse as his intellectual interests were, he appears to have been anything but a dry-as-dust. Though as a logician he had trained himself severely in precision of speech, the hesitating and half-frozen way of talking that most exact thinkers fall into, he seems to have escaped. We have a letter written about this time by a canon named Fulcus, who, dwelling on Abelard's intellectual cleverness, his power and subtlety of expression, makes special mention of the sweetness of his eloquence; *limpidissimus philosophiæ fons*, he calls him, too—philosophy's very clearest fountain. He was not only an easy and agreeable speaker, he had also the advantages of an attractive presence; he was a fine-looking man, in the prime of life.

Now for about twenty years he had been a hero of the schools. The philosophic and theological leaders of the age he had overthrown and trampled on; the audiences that he had been at the first successful in drawing had steadily increased. Established in Paris without controversy, a canon of the church, in the chair of Notre-Dame, the philosophical throne of France, he lectured to the best pupils of Europe. Fulcus, in his letter to Abelard, described the geographical extent of his influence thus:

> "Rome sent her sons to be taught by you, the former teacher of all arts confessing herself not so wise as you. No distance, no height of mountains, no depth of valleys, no road hard to travel or perilous with robbers, hindered scholars from hastening to you. The English students were not frightened by the tempestuous waves of the sea between; every peril was despised as soon as your name was known. The remote Britons, the Angevins, the Picts, the Gascons, the Spaniards, the people of Normandy and Flanders, the Teutons, and the Suevi, all about Paris and through France, near and remote, thirsted to be taught by you, as if they could learn nowhere else."

Such eminence had not come to him without effort. He had been a close worker, secluding himself from society. "The assiduity of my application to study," he says, "prevented my associating with refined ladies, and I had hardly any acquaintance with women outside of the church." The purity of his morals was only less famous than his intellect; he says that the notion of associating, as many churchmen of the time did, with coarse women was odious to him.

But suddenly over this man already middle-aged, and, as one might suppose, established in self-control mentally and physically, there came a reaction. Reputation had become an old story, his enthusiasm for philosophy seemed to dwindle when he believed himself the first philosopher of the world; no doubt, too, the intellectual pressure of his work had so worn upon him as to make a change of interests impulsive. So Abelard turned to divert himself with immoral indulgences, and at thirty-eight began the life of passion.

Several years before this, a story had begun to circulate that another canon of Notre-Dame, Fulbert by name, had a remarkable niece. She was then only a little girl in a nunnery at Argenteuil, but year by year the accounts of her precocity grew more astonishing, and by the time she was sixteen we are told that she was talked about through the whole kingdom. This was Heloise, and her uncle—people did not know whether he was prouder or fonder of her. He brought her back to his own house near the cathedral, and Abelard met her to find the reports of her learning had not been exaggerated, and—something more interesting—to find that she was not merely a scholar, that she was a genius. The modern accounts of this famous story that I have seen (most of them mere imitations of one or two authors who really have taken the trouble to study the originals) declare that Heloise was uncommonly beautiful, but there seems to be no authority for this. Abelard says only, "*per faciem non infirma*"—"not lowest in beauty, but in literary culture highest." Making allowance for his rhetorical contrast, we may say, without intensives, that she was attractive as well as brilliant.

We should have to read a good many indecent chronicles, and get thoroughly familiar with Don Juan prototypes, to find as cold-blooded a story of seduction as this that follows. We have it from Abelard's own pen, told in perfectly calm language, a clear-cut narrative without the slightest tremor of confession about it. He was delighted with her loveliness, her youth and innocence, her fame, and most of all with her brilliancy. He says that he believed no woman whom he might honor with his regard could resist the combination of his personal qualities and his reputation. But he wished cultivated, congenial companionship in his amours, and deliberately resolved to betray this girl of sixteen under the disguise of her teacher. At his own application, Fulbert received him as a lodger, the board to be paid by private instruction of his niece. "He gave the lamb to me, a wolf"—such is Abelard's well-chosen metaphor. She was to be taught at any hours, day or night, that her tutor found convenient. She was to obey him in everything, and if he thought fit it was enjoined upon him to discipline her with the rod. "To such an extent," Abelard remarks, "was he blinded by his trust in his niece, and by my reputation for strict morality."

Nothing could be more repulsive than the coldly deliberate wickedness of Abelard's plan, and it would be time thrown away to attempt any extenuation of it. But the crime once committed, it is a relief to find something in addition to brute passion present in the unscrupulous seducer. The girl who had fascinated him, won from him as complete love as his nature was capable of giving. Week by week he resigned himself more and more to his happiness, he neglected the school, his lectures were only the repetition of formerly acquired views, and he wooed philosophy for no new truths. Even the perfunctory teaching that he did grew irksome to him, and his knowledge of the great sadness, groans, and lamentations that he tells arose among his followers, was powerless to break the spell. For it was only a spell: he was pre-eminently an intellectual man with superficial affections; his heart was given to philosophy, and the only permanent passion of his life was ambition. But little as the praise is, to that little extent it is to his credit that where he had planned for himself a holiday from mental and moral severity, in which he was to enjoy relaxation selfishly and viciously at Heloise's undivided cost, he found his better nature captured by this loveliest representative of womanhood in its fullest and most exceptional combination of elements that mediæval history has made known to us.

After all, Abelard was not wholly destitute of the moral sensibilities: I believe no narrator of this story has called attention to his love for his old home in Brittany, or to his family's devotion to him and reliance on his guidance, or to the tenderness with which he mentions his mother. In spite of all the viciousness in his early and the hardness in his later treatment of Heloise, we may credit him with real affection for her, from the early days of his crime.

For a man of Abelard's force and finish of mind, such a refined companionship must have been the first of pleasures. There are traditions, not to be accepted too credulously, that Heloise was a larger scholar than her lover, and could read Hebrew and Greek—those rarest accomplishments of mediæval learning. That at least she knew Latin literature well, we have abundant evidence, and the most positive proof that her scholarship was refined and appreciative, that she felt poetry as well as understood it. Her mind responded also to the theological interests of the thinkers of the age, she was at home in the church fathers, and learned from Abelard the main principles of his philosophical doctrine. In trying to conceive a character when information is so fragmentary as ours here, we are no doubt in some danger of making fanciful biography. Three letters of her own, several of Abelard's to her, and his autobiography, a few slight contemporary hints—these materials leave some important points of her character undeveloped. But given certain suggestions, our imaginative instincts cannot go far wrong, provided the inferences of sympathetic interpretation are held in check by judgment. These guides teach us to see in the girl Heloise an extraordinary combination of thoughtfulness and bright temper, active thinking and religious deference, accurate scholarship (after the fashion of mediæval schools) and æsthetic sensibility, passion and maidenly delicacy. To this last quality Abelard has borne complete testimony, and her own letters supply any evidence needed. Absorbed though her whole nature was in her love, her lover himself has let us know that her modesty had to be conquered more than once by blows.

Her mind was mastered by the greatness of his reputation, her eye was taken with his beauty, her imagination was fascinated by his universal charm: it is no wonder that she was flattered and bewitched into loving him. But the completeness and devotion and ecstatic self-oblivion of the love she gave him is a wonder. Her generous faith, though to an undeserving object, communicates to the ineffective results of her life an ideal value; by a supreme self-forgetting, she rendered herself worthy to be always remembered.

Abelard's was a stormy life in a stormy age, when the scholars fought quite as bitterly as the soldiers, and the last forty-four years of Heloise's life were the tragedy of being buried alive, unable to die. But for a few months in this year 1118, both found perfect happiness. We have a pretty picture outlined for us of the way their time went. Abelard says: "We used to have our books open, but we talked more of love than about the reading, there were more kisses than ideas. Love made pictures of each of us in the other's eyes more often than we turned our eyes upon the books."

Every now and then this great philosopher appeared in a new rôle. As to most of the highest men, Nature had given him a great deal more than brains. He had a wonderfully fine voice, was fond of music, and as poets in those days went, he was a poet. He had stopped constructing dialectics, but his mind could not be inactive; so he took up the art of song-writing and song-making, and wrote love-lyrics and many of them, almost all directly in the praise of Heloise. Nor was he content to praise her to her own ears alone; the man was past all prudence in the violence of his new absorption. He let others hear them, and no doubt his hateful egotism was flattered by the thought that the most fascinating girl in all France would thus become known as his mistress. The lyrics at once caught the popular fancy; we hear of them as spreading over the country, sung everywhere by the light-minded. Many years later, Heloise wrote that if any woman's heart could have resisted Abelard's other magic, to read his songs and to hear him sing them would surely have conquered her.

The neglect of his work, and the notoriety of these love-ditties after a while made public Abelard's real relation to his pupil. Yet for some time after the world at large understood it, the devoted uncle and guardian of the girl heard nothing, and after the rumors did begin to reach him, he obstinately refused to believe them. Nothing in the whole history shows the essential goodness of Heloise more significantly than the canon Fulbert's complete incredulity; for as the event proved, his nature was not so gentle as to repudiate harsh thoughts without the strongest prepossessions. When the truth was forced upon him, his distress was so intense that even the cold-hearted Abelard was compelled to pity him. But if Abelard pitied the uncle, how much greater his distress for the niece, and greater still, unfortunately, his apprehension for himself. Egotist he proved himself, but he proved himself also Heloise's real lover. "First we lived together in one house," he says, "but at last in one soul." In the crash of public disgrace, "neither of us complained of personal suffering, but each for the suffering that came to the other," and the bodily separation that ensued, he says with a touch of real feeling, was "the greatest linking of our souls."

Soon after the separation, Abelard discovered that Heloise required more care and comforts than the heart-broken and embittered Fulbert would be likely to provide, and he devised and carried through a plan to take her back to his own country, to his sister's house. There, amid the scenes of her lover's boyhood, in that Brittany whose legend and poetry have blessed us with so many of our loveliest romances, this heroine of a deeper romance than any of fiction found a home for several months. We may guess that the home was pleasant to her, for the lady with whom she lived afterwards entered the abbey of which Heloise was prioress. Abelard meanwhile was continuing his lectures in Paris, fearing—he seems to have been at all times a great deal of a coward—the personal violence from Heloise's family which the fierce habits of the age gave him reason to anticipate. At last the distress of Fulbert touched his better feeling into the wish to give him comfort, this long separation from Heloise he found hard to support, and his fear of revenge constantly increased. These motives induced a promise to rectify his offence by marriage. He made only one condition—that the marriage should be secret.

On the whole, this is perhaps the most favorable exhibition of himself that Abelard ever made. With all deductions for selfish considerations, it is reasonable to allow some weight to moral feeling, and a good deal more to devotion for the girl. This renders it all the sadder to find him some sixteen years later referring to this best act of his life with a feeble apology. "Let no one," he entreats, "wonder at my offer of marriage, who has felt the power of love, and known how the greatest men have been overthrown by woman."

Even here when his feeling for Heloise seems strongest, we see that his selfish ambition was stronger still. Secular as his tastes were, bound to the church by his intellectual side only, he still hoped to rise to ecclesiastical dignities and power. From very early times the disposition for a celibate clergy had been strong, and five years before Abelard's birth Hildebrand had declared that no married priest should have any part in the celebration of the mass. Quite apart from all questions of marriage, Abelard seems to have had scarcely any chance of distinguished clerical dignity; the student crowds might follow him, but the leaders of the church were dead set against his rationalism; they feared and hated the arrogant and progressive thinker. If Abelard had acted like a man, and had openly chosen married love with the girl whose mind and heart were, either of them, better than the best of life's other gifts, the misfortunes of his distressed later career might have been avoided, and Heloise, after a happy and lovely life, would be no more remembered to-day than the flowers she had gathered, or the birds she heard sing. But because the man, not quite unprincipled, was yet not true, he brought death upon his own good name, and upon Heloise a melancholy life with which she paid too dear for all the remembrance and love that the ages have given her. To his selfishness we owe the sweetest and saddest story which the middle ages have bequeathed us; but we think of the words of Demodocus, as he recites in the Odyssey the story of heroes dead: "This the gods contrived, and for these they ordained destruction, so that the people of times to come might have a song."

His mind once made up, Abelard started for Brittany, to see the son of whose birth he had just heard, and to take back the mother as his bride. But when this resolution was known to Heloise, he met an unexpected opposition. She said she did not wish him to marry her, and persisted in her refusal.

Unwomanly does it appear, this unwillingness of Heloise to become her lover's wife? She knew Abelard's vehement ambition, the impossibility of its being satisfied if he was known to be a married man, the practical certainty that her family would prefer the redemption of her reputation to her husband's success. So she told Abelard that to marry her would be dangerous to him,—but still more, that it would be disgraceful. She talked to him in the rôle of a learned and ascetic mediæval preacher; she seems to draw a monk's rough robe about her girlish figure, to disguise her tones, and to muffle her bright face in a cowl. We have long, formally rendered objections, a crowd of citations from the Bible, Cicero, Theophrastus, Jerome, Josephus, Augustine,—to prove marriage less honorable than celibacy, devotion to knowledge a duty not to be interfered with by the responsibilities and annoyances of a family, conformity to the rules of the church the highest obligation. Her desire for his own greatness completely overshadows her passion for his love. He is already the first of philosophers, but if he has outrivalled others, he must go on to surpass himself. For this, he must have quiet and solitude, freedom for thought. She quotes a Roman maxim that all things are to be neglected for philosophy. What monks endure through love of God, the thinker ought to endure from devotion to truth. If laymen and gentiles have lived thus continently, bound by no religious profession, what does it become a clerk and a canon to do? "If you regard not God, at least care for philosophy."

"For what harmony is there," she asks, "between a scholar and a nurse, a writing-desk and a cradle, books and spinning-wheels? Who when absorbed in religious or philosophic meditation can endure hearing children cry, or having to listen to the lullabies of the woman who soothes them? Rich people can get along, for they have abundant room and plenty of servants; but scholars are not rich." She has difficulty in keeping herself disguised: in the excess of her feeling she throws out her arms, and discloses the gracious outline of the unselfish woman. Then, after reasoning, come personal pleadings. Is he sacrificing himself for her? She is content as she is. Now she holds him by the free gift of that love and favor to which he would have a claim in marriage. Does he believe she feels herself disgraced by this relation? To be called his mistress is dear and ennobling to her. Years later when she was past her middle life, she wrote to Abelard that "the name of mistress, or even of harlot, was sweeter to me then the holier name of wife, so that by my greater humiliation I might gain greater favor and less injure thy fame. I call God to witness that if Augustus would have set me by himself at the head of the whole world, it would have seemed to me more dear and noble to be called thy mistress than his empress."

Thus by argument, authority, protestation that her sacrifice is choice, she tries to conquer his decision. Nay, she throws aside the cowl entirely, and by her natural bright humor tries to banter him into acquiescence. "And then think," she says in substance, "what a plague a wife is to a man. Only imagine" (and she laughs, and Abelard laughs too, at the inconceivable grotesqueness of the idea), "imagine what a shrew I might turn out! I might treat you as Xanthippe treated *her* philosopher." She reminds him of the passage where Jerome tells the story about Socrates' wife having fretted and scolded and raged one day through the house with desperate temper, until she wound up by throwing a basin of dirty water over him:

"He took it patiently, and wiped his head:'Rain follows thunder,'—that was all he said."

To Abelard's credit, this impassioned unselfishness strengthened, instead of weakening, his resolution. Heloise was forced to yield, but her instincts saw the dark shadows gathering about them: with sobs and tears she exclaimed, "In the ruin of both of us not less pain is to follow than was the love that came before."

Leaving the child with his aunt the lovers returned to Paris; there they were married in great secrecy, and at once separated. After this they met but seldom, and then with careful precautions against their interviews becoming known. Heloise's family, however, as she had feared, determined to redeem her good name by announcing that Abelard had made her honorable reparation. When people came to her and asked if it was really true that she was the canon's wife, she denied the story angrily. When her uncle and other relatives contradicted her contradiction, the girl took religion's holiest name in vain, in her asseverations that Abelard was not her husband. Fulbert lost all patience, and attempted by cruelty and indignity to drive her to confess the truth. She told Abelard of what she suffered, and one night he contrived to steal her away from her uncle and to carry her back to her old nunnery at Argenteuil, where she assumed most of the dress of the order, and received only occasional visits from him.

The conjecture that Abelard designed to keep her there, and as soon as his attachment could be weaned to make her take the vows and thus save himself from all further trouble, suggests itself to us to-day: with greater force, it occurred to the people immediately concerned. The rage of the uncle and his friends at Abelard's treachery, first and last, to themselves, and at his heartlessness toward the girl whose worth they understood so well, grew uncontrollable; they bribed a servant to admit them to his house by night, and avenged themselves.

Abelard's spirit was broken, as he saw all hopes of ecclesiastical promotion at an end, and his fame turned to notoriety. Heretofore his public appearances had made the sensation of a king's: "What region did not burn to see you!" asked Heloise. "Who, when you walked abroad, did not hurry to look at you, rising on tiptoe and with straining eyes?" But now every look he fancied scornful.

In this wild age there was always one refuge for the victims of the world or of themselves. To the monasteries flocked all classes, from fashionable knights broken down or unsuccessful or weary of conflict, to the half-witted clowns sheltered and utilized as lay-brethren. Husbands forsook their wives, and wives fled from their husbands, to take shelter in the religious life. In this early part of the twelfth century, monastic houses were multiplying like hives of bees, constantly sending out from themselves colonies that quickly became parents of others. For some time the tendency had been to an easier discipline than the traditional, but at last asceticism had blazed out anew, and the rich and luxurious Cluny paled in popularity before Clairveaux or the Grande Chartreuse. In this single century the Cistercians expanded from one abbey to eight hundred, a single one of which is said to have controlled seven hundred benefices. The one meal a day, the hard manual labor, the restricted sleep, the wearisome routine of prayer, reading, and penance, won by their very severity and by the mystical impression of sanctity and immortal safety which brooded about these retired prisons of self-condemned sin.

"Oh, hide me in your gloom profound, Ye solemn seats of holy pain,"

was the cry with which multitudes approached the gates that should emancipate them from a freedom which did not satisfy. Ben Jonson's fear lest his inclination to God might be

"Through weariness of life, not love of thee,"

was realized in the case of numbers of convertites quite equalling and probably far exceeding those who entered the ascetic orders from the enthusiasm of visionaries. To this retirement, as a screen from the world's curiosity and fancied mocks, Abelard now resolved to withdraw, as his father and mother in their later lives had done before him. His jealousy could not leave Heloise behind, so he told her of his purpose, and hoped that she would volunteer to imitate him. But Heloise made no such offer. In every way hers was a mind beyond her age, and the unnatural harshness of cloistral discipline, its artificial dreariness, its "hope to merit heaven by making earth a hell," seemed to her fine insight untrue. Though she had suffered, she was yet in tune with life; her heart assured her that innocent pleasure is the soul's hymn of praise to God; bitterly as she shared her husband's misery, she saw no reason for separating her life and his; most of all, she revolted from the notion of professing religion with lip-service only. But Abelard urged, insisted, even commanded, and, seeing it to be his wish, the girl-wife yielded. She told herself that only she was responsible for her husband's afflictions; except for her, his prosperity would have continued undimmed; so the day was fixed on which, in her old nunnery, she should take the vows of perpetual seclusion.

It must have been a strange scene in that chapel at Argenteuil. Abelard was there, still in his habit of a mere secular priest, there to make sure that Heloise's impulses should not burst out again, and cast her back into the world's sunshine. The bishop, attended by his priests, stands at the altar: upon it lies a newly consecrated veil. The nuns, kneeling in their accustomed places, are praying. All wait for the votaress, but she is detained by a crowd of friends. There were many of them there, as Abelard has told us, and they could not endure that this girl, personally so charming, perhaps the most accomplished intellectually of all the women of France, should consummate the sacrifice that she had already in such large measure made. They knew her love for the bright things of life, her beautiful zest for the joyous and sympathetic, her eagerness in study, the grace of her strong, sweet seriousness. Such a nature might be for a time bewildered at the loss of the love of one of the most famous men living, yet if for a little while they could keep her face unhidden by the veil, she might forget. So they delay her outside the chapel, pleading with a heart that has made the same pleas for itself before. Presently the door is pushed open and she enters the oratory, her friends still about her. Even in the sacred place they continue their entreaties, and Abelard's glance is anxiously upon her; but her eyes are downcast. "How they pitied her!" he has told us; "they kept trying to hold back her youth from the yoke of monastic rule, as from punishment intolerable." The bishop seems half pitiful, half impatient; the nuns look up from their praying. Has the world renewed its hold upon her? Will she snatch herself from God? Does he no longer attract her? At this last moment is she hesitating?

She was hesitating; the world did have a hold upon her. God? God had never attracted her.

In all the ceremonials of the Catholic Church, there can have been none which has so combined sacrilege with loftiness of feeling as did the scene which followed. From the silent, even wistful hearing that she has been giving to her friends, Heloise suddenly starts away, and, as if waking from a reverie, she moves with dreamy gesture toward her husband. Her lips part, and what will be her last words as a lady of the world? Some scriptural exhortation to her friends to follow her as she follows Christ? A cry of exultant renunciation of the wilds of life's ocean, and of contentment at the holy calm in the bosom of the church?

The girl is weeping, and as she tries to control herself to speak, her misery overcomes her, and she bursts into loud sobs. But it must have been surprising to the listening ecclesiastics to hear the words which at last got expression. It is probably the only time in the church's history that a novice has taken her last vows with the prelude of a quotation from a love speech in a pagan poem, directing it not to the bleeding effigy of her present and eternal Master hanging above the altar, but to a human lover at her side. Heloise "broke out as she could between her tears and sobs," in a passage from one of the later books of Lucan's *Pharsalia*: surely as she spoke the lines, her voice grew steady, and her eyes looked bravely through the tears:

"Husband and lord, too worthy for my bed,Can Fortune thus cast down so dear a head?Fated to make thee wretched, why did IBecome thy wife? Accept the penalty;I will endure it gladly."

I fancy that Abelard was quite as much impressed by the brilliant young mind that could make so apt and scholarly a quotation from the Roman classics, as by the heart which dared on the very margin of the altar to fling back to the world and up to God this protestation of its unfaltering human love, which took the vows of religion from no other motive than to impose torture upon itself—an offering not to God, but to Abelard.

As she spoke the verses, she hurried to the altar. *Accipe pœnas, quas sponte luam,*—her voice died away, the bishop received her, and covered her forever with the veil.

Heloise was only eighteen.

The convent gates shut in all sight of her for the next ten or eleven years. But in 1130, the nunnery over which she had become prioress was broken up by the unfavorable decision of a suit for the land and buildings which it occupied. This decade had brought abundant misery to Abelard. His heresies in theology had been exposed, and he had been compelled to burn a treasured book in which they were expounded, a council had imprisoned him in an abbey where it was boasted that his haughtiness was tamed by a course of vigorous whipping administered under the abbot's supervision.

There is something pitiful in the thought of such physical and mental pride being under the control of fanatical monks, ignorant and coarse, from whom he was glad to escape to a desert east of Troyes, as a hermit. He had taught at intervals during these years, and once for a season with a notable renewal of his early success. Near Troyes, where he had built his hermit-shelter out of reeds and stubble, in a desolate region infested by wild animals and a covert for robbers, some vagrant student found the intellectual champion, and reported at Paris his discovery. The news spread, and soon the desert was populous. The students built a house for the master, apparently a commodious one, and about it they made more temporary structures for their own shelter. Not only the younger class of scholars besieged him for instruction; older men, ecclesiastics who, as we are told, were wont to grasp instead of giving, paid generously toward constructing a home for the great philosopher. But he was world-weary, and soon retired again to a bleak monastery on the Atlantic, in the lower part of Brittany, where he became abbot of a set of half-barbarous monks, who resented his austere rule and, so he tells us, tried repeatedly to poison him because he interfered with their profligacy. While there he had learned of Heloise's loss of her nunnery, and had established her and her religious sisters in the buildings in Champagne that had been standing unoccupied since he broke up that last school. "The Paraclete," he had called the home, as a special invocation to the Holy Spirit and as a tribute for the temporary comfort that he received there. Possibly he himself conducted his wife thither, but it is equally likely that he did not see her after he forced her into the church.

For ten years he appears to have struggled on in Brittany, with no intellectual associations, none of the notoriety with which he had been so long pampered, in terror for his life, yet still working at his philosophy of religion. At last he was impelled to talk of what he had endured and was still enduring; to speak in the bitterness of his soul, and get, perhaps, the consolation of pity. He composed a long and immensely interesting autobiography, telling the whole story of his youth, his later triumphs, his logical acumen, his love, his disgrace, the injustice of his condemnation by the conservative church, the tumult of his experiences in the lonely monastery of St. Gildas. The creditable pages are calmly written, the shameful unflinchingly. He tells how tremendous had been his love for Heloise, but he says nothing of loving her still. The narrative reveals an egotist, but it reveals as certainly one of the most striking characters of the Middle Ages.

We find ourselves inevitably speculating upon the life of Heloise during the sixteen or more years whose only recorded event is her removal from

Argenteuil to the Paraclete. It might be that a reaction in her love would follow, when the grim captivity that she had dreaded so became yet more hateful in its realization; she might lose her old gentleness; it might become hopeless for her to try to adjust her spirit to its new conditions and to devote herself to even a submissive piety. From contemporary testimony we are sure that some of these possibilities did not come true. She won respect and even devotion as an abbess, her house prospered financially to her husband's undisguised surprise and admiration, her life was pure from the least fleck of reproach, or criticism in any quarter. May we go farther, and say that her spirit did adjust itself to its new conditions, and lose its pain in a submissive piety? For such a result we should find many parallels in mediæval religion; numerous accounts not to be cavilled at as legendary prove that in these monasteries souls which had suffered found peace. Nay, many a nun among these most refined groups of mediæval women, driven in one way or another to forsake the hope of love and earthly happiness, secured delight of heart in a sort of spiritual romance. As their emotion grew more subtilized, as asceticism burned away material impulse, some of the gentlest and most poetically endowed of these religious recluses acquired a mystical compensation for their loneliest sacrifice of life,—a divinely idealized personal love, too magical for friendship, too impassioned and mutual for worship, where, the sexes mysteriously spiritualized, translated womanhood should rest at last on the breast of Christ. The final vow of religious consecration was the nun's betrothal to the divine man; to make herself beautiful for his bride she wasted her body by fasting and scarred it with the scourge; the rough lath cross on the wall of her cell was his love token; love messages came from him in her dreams; prostrated on the chapel flagging she indited to him prayers that scarcely needed verse to become lyrics. And when to such a mystic's contemplation the cloister sanctity seemed too worldly, when her exhausted body found the walk from cell to chapel too long a journey and she was compelled to stay in the coffin that for years of nights had sweetly reminded her of the sure untwining of soul and sense, when she could hear only faintly her sisters' thin chanting of the hours, and felt her spirit quivering with new sensations, vague, awed, and eager, she understood that the waiting time was over, and her espousal at hand. Her failing eyes see white processionals that come to lead her to the banqueting house where the banner of His love shall be over her; the music, which the dying so often hear, for her is a marriage melody ringing from angelic harps and dulcimers; with new-born strength and grace, mantled in new raiment, she floats upward to her desire. And when space has been traversed the immortal vision bursts upon her, a great poet has put in words her last thought this side heaven:

"He lifts me to the golden doors,The flashes come and go;All heaven bursts her starry floors,And strows her light below,And deepens on and up! the gatesRoll back, and far withinFor me the Heavenly Bridegroom waits,To make me pure of sin.The sabbaths of Eternity,One sabbath deep and wide,—A light upon the shining sea,The Bridegroom with his bride."

But for Heloise there was no such resource. It is to natures more ethereal and constitutionally religious that such fancies and dreams appeal. The main feature of the matured Heloise is sanity and balanced womanhood; she was too strong and intense to be a sentimentalist. Could the nature which had once been caught into the clouds by the whirlwind of love, beguile itself from the memory of that storm of rapture by a visionary tempest raised with a fan? And yet there would be some satisfaction if we could conceive her adjusting herself to the spiritual life with closer accord, and passing even through the gates of superstitious hallucination from the harsh religion of her day into the inner sanctuary whose "solemn shadow is better than the sun," finding an outlet for her quick emotions in this personal love for her new Master.

Heloise had been a nun some sixteen years when some one showed her Abelard's so-called *Historia Calamitatum*. Apparently her husband had forbidden her to write to him; but though she had kept a long silence, she was a lover until death. This account of Abelard's sufferings and perils broke her constraint; she could not help writing to comfort him and to beg for news of his safety. What other love-letters equal the intensity, the tenderness, the womanliness of these final appeals for the broken love? Through their nervous pliancy one may learn as nowhere else the reality of Browning's

"Infinite passion, and the painOf finite hearts that yearn."

In them appears also her strength of nature; they are the love-calls of a woman who knows that the man she continues to set far above all the rest of humanity is wronging her. She chides him for this long and complete neglect, but there is a marvellous sweetness in her caressing reproaches. She tells him to remember under what peculiar bonds she holds him,—what sacred obligation of marriage, of love, and of devotion he owes to her; she gave her honor to please him, not herself; she sacrificed her tender age to the harshness of a monastic life not from piety, but only in submission to his desire. "There was a time," she writes, "when people doubted whether in our amour I yielded to love or to passion. But the end shows how I began; to please you, I have denied myself all pleasures." She points out to him how differently the end interprets his feeling for her. "It is common talk," she says, "that you felt only gross emotions toward me, and when there was a stop to their indulgence, your so-called love vanished. My dearest one, would that this appeared to me only, and not to every one; would that I might be soothed by hearing others excuse you, or that I could myself devise excuses."

She appears to entertain no hope that he will visit her, though she hints longingly at the possibility; but he can at least do as much for her as he does for others under obligations so far slighter, as much as the example of the church fathers regarding the women of their flocks teaches him to do,—he can write and tell her how he is, he can comfort her love: or (and she appeals to the monk who may listen, even if the old-time lover will not) he can send spiritual admonition to uphold her slipping soul. Her heart put at rest, she can be so much freer for the divine service. "When you wooed me for the pleasures of earth," she reminds him, "you sent me letter after letter; with many songs you put your Heloise in the speech of all, so that every street and house echoed with me. How much more ought you now to excite toward God the one whom then you aroused to sin."

She tells him again of her complete absorption in him: "You are the only one who can make me either sad or happy; you only can be my comforter. The whole world knows how much I loved you," and she turns with a half-shuddering reminiscence to the day she became a nun. "It was for you, not for God—that sacrifice. From God I can look for no reward; consider, then, how vain my trial, if by it I win nothing from you"; and the woman for sixteen years a nun calls God—and remember that hers was the God of mediæval superstition—to witness that she would have followed Abelard, or gone before him, if she had seen him hastening to hell.

Her letters evidently moved the monk, for his replies were full of good advice, and under the surface gave some indications of tender regard. But the affection that we find is colorless and formal. No word of a husband's gentleness, nor warmth of phrase, not a hint that he cherishes happy memories of the old days of their union. They are the letters of an old man, absorbed in himself, worn by the world, who has no capacity for anything deeper than kind feeling. He calls her his sister, once dear in the world, now dearer in Christ, begs her prayers for him living and dead, and entreats that whenever he may die she will have his body carried to her abbey, that the constant sight of his grave may move her and her spiritual daughters to pray for his salvation. He gulps down the *Lachrima Christi* of her exquisite love as if it were the small beer of pietistic commonplace, and then looks disappointed to find that it was not. For he ignores the soul of her letters, and composes complacent treatises of twelfth-century ecclesiastical discipline designed to subject her to a mechanical and lifeless asceticism.

Heloise in answer reproaches him for his talk of death, like a brave heart bidding him not by anticipation suffer before his time. The knowledge of her husband's unhappiness is a renewed affliction, and she owns that there is nothing but sorrow in her life. Like a daring Titaness, she exclaims against God's administration of his world:

> "While we lived in sin, he indulged us; when we married, he forced us to separate. Let his other creatures rejoice and count themselves safe from the inclement clemency of the God whom I almost dare to call cruel to me in every way. They are safe, for upon me he has used up all the weapons of his wrath, so that he has none with which to rage at others; nor, if any remained, could he find a place in me wherein to strike them."

After sixteen years' silence, this woman has broken into speech, and unmasked confessions of her inner spirit will no longer be restrained. She goes on as if carried by cyclone winds; she tells her far-off lover what few nuns under terror of eternal death can ever have brought themselves to confide to their confessors in scarcely audible whisper. She calls up the scenes of their union; she confesses that visions of that life are with her constantly: she bemoans the thoughts which "haunt me sometimes, even at the holy mass." She was no calm northern woman; she had nothing of the temperament that Shakespeare compared to an icicle

"That's curdied by the frost from purest snow,And hangs on Dian's temple";

she was made to walk with love, under summer moonlight,—no sister of Percivale, to forget thwarted desire in prayer beneath the frosty stars of winter.

"Help me," cries this victim of a gloomy religion, "for I do not find how by penance to appease God, whom I still accuse of the greatest cruelty. It is easy to confess and to torture the body; it is hard to tear the soul from its desires. My mind keeps the same wish for sin; so sweet was our happiness that I cannot be sorry for it. Most wretched life, if I have endured so much in vain, destined to have no recompense hereafter."

Thus Heloise the woman and Heloise the abbess fight out the old problem whether the training of life is by the use of its gifts, or by the rejection of them; shall we play the full organ, or only the harsh reed stops? The church taught her to condemn what nature taught her to justify. The religious authority of all the dark ages confronted this woman's instincts of life, and—to her honor—it could not quell them. Yet conceive her wretchedness and the anguish of her mental struggle, living as she did in the middle of Catholic mediævalism. When, after a scanty rest, she left her cell at midnight, this artificial conscience attended her to the long chapel service that followed, pointed at the austere pages over which she bent in the study when the service was over, kept calling her hypocrite as she chided and instructed the nuns whom she is said to have ruled so wisely, snatched food and wine from her hungry lips, with fast, pitiless lashing wielded the whip of penance, haunted her sleep with its stern face. Yet the pleasures of time were still honorable to her; the world *was* good; her love *had* been beautiful; if her conscience prayed forgiveness for it, her heart sang, because she had known it.

To hear this bewildered voice crying to Abelard for his prayers because in spite of the world's praise of her virtue she thinks herself a hypocrite,—Oh, my only one, pray for me, for I cannot be sorry that we loved—to hear this makes one glad that the time has passed for identifying the devil with the world's laughter, and God with its sobbing.

She lived on as abbess of the Paraclete for twenty-one years after she buried her husband. We cannot believe that as one set of feelings cooled with age, her spiritual emotions grew more impulsive. In the twenty-eight years which followed her last letter to Abelard, she no doubt more and more mechanically went through the life of monastic duty, her intellectual accord with the church leading her to an increasingly calm performance of routine piety, her heart more and more silent—but never dead. We fancy its main utterance an anticipation of that cry of Clough's—"Submit, submit." Thus kindling with no spiritual ardor—(she once confessed that her religious ambition did not rise so high as to wish a crown of victory, or to have God's strength made perfect in her weakness), she lived out her faithful and successful life as abbess of the Paraclete, comforted—we may hope—by a continuance of the intellectual consolations of her youth, and honored, as we know, by church and world. If imaginary biography is ever safe we may employ it here, and fancy that when she came to die she repeated what she had said years before, that she should be quite content to be given just a corner in heaven. I think as she lay waiting to be received there, she dreamed of looking up from it, not at the ineffable glory, but at one human face stationed highest among the masters in divine philosophy. Highest among the masters! Less than a hundred and fifty years later, the great poem of mediævalism forgot to give Abelard a place even among the penitents of purgatory, and to-day except by special students he is remembered only as Heloise's unworthy lover.

APPENDIX.

At the suggestion of the publishers the following brief notices of some of the works and authors mentioned in these essays are added for convenience of reference.

ÆTHIOPICA, the oldest and most famous of the Greek romances. It narrates the loves of Theagenes and Charicleia, and was written in his youth by Heliodorus of Emesa, who flourished about the end of the fourth century, and died as Bishop of Tricca in Thessaly.

ALEXANDER, or as he is termed in some MSS. the Wild Alexander. A South-German poet of the thirteenth century. Of his life scarcely anything is known.

CHRESTIEN DE TROYES, a French trouvère, who flourished in the second half of the twelfth century. He may be regarded as the popularizer in the French form of the cycle of tales that centre about the Round Table. The most important of his poems is the one bearing the title, *Perceval le Gallois* or *Li Contes del Graal*.

COMTE DE CHAMPAGNE.—See Thibaut.

ARNAUD DANIEL, a Provençal poet, who died about 1189. He was distinguished for the complicated character of his versification, and in particular was the inventor of the verse called the *sestine*. He lived for some time at the court of Richard I. of England. Dante in the twenty-sixth canto of the *Purgatory* puts him at the head of all the Provençal poets. He was also highly praised by Petrarch.

DAPHNIS AND CHLOE, a Greek pastoral romance, the prototype of all the pastoral romances which have been written in various languages. Its composition is usually ascribed to a certain Longus, a Greek sophist, who flourished about the beginning of the fifth century.

FREIDANK, the composer of a Middle High German didactic poem, which belongs to the first half of the thirteenth century. The name has been considered by some to be merely allegorical. His work, which was entitled *Bescheidenheit*, consists of over four thousand verses and discusses religious, political and social questions. It was an exceedingly popular work during the Middle Ages.

GACES BRULLES, a French trouvère of the early part of the thirteenth century. He was born in Champagne, but spent a portion of his life in Brittany. About seventy of his *chansons* are extant.

GOTTFRIED VON STRASSBURG, a German poet who flourished at the end of the twelfth and the beginning of the thirteenth century. His great work was the epic entitled *Tristan und Isolde*, continued by others after his death. This took place somewhere between 1210 and 1220. Gottfried wrote also many lyric poems.

GUILLAUME DE BALAUN (or BALAZUN), a Provençal poet of the twelfth century. He was the lover of the lady of Joviac, in the Gévaudan. Alienation having sprung up between them upon account of his assumed or real indifference, his mistress would not restore him to favor unless he should agree to extract the nail of the longest finger of his right hand, and should come and present it to her with a poem composed expressly for the occasion. The condition was fulfilled.

JOHANN HADLAUB, a German poet, who flourished at the end of the thirteenth and the beginning of the fourteenth century. His life was spent mainly in Zurich. His compositions were principally love-songs and popular songs dealing with the pleasures of autumn and harvest. A statue was erected to him in Zurich in 1885.

HARTMANN VON AUE, a Middle High German, belonging by birth to a noble Swabian family, was born about 1170, and died between 1210 and 1220. He wrote *Erec and Enide*, basing it upon the French poem with the same title of Chrestien de Troyes. Another poem of his belonging also to the Arthurian cycle is *Iwein*. The most popular of his works with modern students is *Der arme Heinrich*. The details of its story have been made known to English readers by Longfellow's *Golden Legend*, which is founded upon it. Another work of his is entitled *Gregorius vom Stein*.

HEINRICH VON MORUNGEN, a German minnesinger, a knight of Thuringia, who flourished at the end of the twelfth and the beginning of the thirteenth century. His last years were spent at the court of Meissen. He wrote many love-songs, many of which owe their existence to those of the troubadours.

HEINRICH VON VELDEKE, a German poet of the twelfth century, who was of a noble family settled near Maastricht, on the lower Rhine. Besides the love-songs and other pieces he wrote, he was the composer of the epic of the *Eneide*, the first poem of the Middle High German epic poetry, which reached its highest development in the writings of Hartmann von Aue, Wolfram von Eschenbach, and Gottfried von Strassburg.

HUGO VON TRIMBERG, a German poet, who flourished at the end of the thirteenth and the beginning of the fourteenth century. From 1260 to 1309 he was rector of the collegiate school in the Theuerstadt, a suburb of Bamberg. He is known as the composer of the *Renner*, a didactic poem, in which the manners and customs of the time are largely depicted, and the prevailing vices severely censured.

JACOPO DA TODI, or JACOPONE, an Italian poet, born about the middle of the thirteenth century at Todi, in the duchy of Spoleto. He belonged to the noble family of the Benedetti, began life as an advocate, but, on account of the sudden accidental death of his wife, devoted himself to a religious life and entered the order of Franciscans. He wrote many religious poems in Italian, and also in Latin. To him in particular is ascribed the composition of the famous *Stabat Mater Dolorosa*.

NEIDHART VON REUENTHAL, a German lyric poet of the thirteenth century. He was of a noble Bavarian family, but spent part of his life in Austria. His poems were written between 1210 and 1240, and are of special interest for the descriptions they give of the customs of the times.

THIBAUT, COUNT OF CHAMPAGNE AND KING OF NAVARRE. He was born at Troyes in 1201, and died in 1253. He is one of the most noted of the early French poets.

ULRICH VON LIECHTENSTEIN, a Middle High German poet, born about 1200, and died in 1276. He was the author of the poem entitled *Frauendienst*, described in this volume, and also of a didactic poem called *Frauenbuch*.

WALTHARIUS ET HILTGUNDE, or simply Waltharius, a Latin poem of the tenth century in hexameter verse, and consisting of between fourteen hundred and fifteen hundred lines. Its authorship is unknown.

WALTHER VON DER VOGELWEIDE, the greatest German poet of the Middle Ages. He was born about 1160, and died about 1230. He was of a knightly family, though poor, and much of his life was spent at the courts of several German princes and emperors. He wrote not only love-poems, but in the contest that went on between the imperialists and the papacy, he supported the side of the former in patriotic verses which had no slight influence upon contemporary opinion. Both for matter and manner he stood at the head of the poets called minnesingers.

WERNHER THE GARDENER, a German poet of the thirteenth century, who composed, between 1234 and 1250, the story of *Meier Helmbrecht*. Nothing is known with certainty of his life.

WOLFRAM VON ESCHENBACH, a German poet, of noble birth, of the latter half of the twelfth century and the beginning of the thirteenth. He died about 1220. His greatest work is the *Parzival*, which was completed about 1210.

It was founded, according to his own statement, partly upon the *Conte del Graal* of Chrestien de Troyes, but more particularly upon the work of a poet whom he calls Kyot, who is supposed by some to be Guyot de Provins, whose romance of *Perceval*, not extant, is assumed to be the original of Wolfram's poem. Another of his poems was the unfinished *Titurel*, which contains the tale of the love of Schionatulander and Sigune.

FOOTNOTES:

[1] *Lit. Fam.*, iv., 1.

[2] Since this passage was written, I have met with the following extract from a letter of Tennyson's, dated in 1874, though with no direct reference to the experience being associated with nature: "All at once, as it were out of the intensity of the consciousness of individuality, the individuality itself has seemed to dissolve and to fade away into boundless being; and this not a confused state, but the clearest of the clearest, the surest of the surest, utterly beyond words, where death was an almost laughable impossibility, the loss of personality (if so it were), seeming no extinction, but the only true life."

[3] Any student of Dante, who recalls his lovely early sonnet, *Guido, vorrei che tu e Lapo ed io*, and compares it with Shelley's almost parallel conception of lovers sailing away in indivisible companionship, in the latter part of *Epipsychidion*, will obtain an excellent illustration of this same difference of feeling about the natural setting for a happy love. In Dante the sentiment is vague, and only what is peaceful, while Shelley's ideal haunt of lovers admits owls and bats with the ring-dove, an "old cavern hoar" left unadorned, mossy mountains, and quivering waves.

[4] We recall his great countryman's modern cry: "Wohin es geht, wer weiss es? Erinnert er sich doch kaum, woher er kam."

[5]

"A woman is never won by what is in one's thoughts: . . . . Of that she can know nothing."

[6] With this extravagant but probably veracious incident, one naturally compares the sacrifice of Guillem de Balaun's finger nail.

[7] These poet lovers seem to have been frequently laughed at. For instance, Pierre Vidal was promised in their amusement anything by the ladies whom he loved. Na Alazais was so indignant when he took encouragement to steal his one kiss, that he was compelled to flee, and go with Richard to the East.

[8] We must remember that the unwillingness of the upper grade of society to have peasants assume its styles of dress, went so far that ducal edicts were issued forbidding them to use coats of mail and helmets, or to carry

any weapons. Bitter complaints were made of their wearing any stuffs so fine as silk, and clothes stylishly cut.

[9]

"La pluye nous a debuez et lavez,Et le soleil dessechez et noirciz;Pies, corbeaulx, nous ont les yeux cavez,Et arrachez la barbe et les sourcilz."

[10] I will not quote Goethe's famous disparagement of the *Divina Commedia*, for the context indicates that it was uttered petulantly. Still, he certainly did not care for Dante, or appreciate him, though he recognized his eminence.

[11] It may be worth noting that Wolfram substitutes for the French original's usual conventionality of a pretty watered meadow, this harder and more appropriate setting.

[12] Tennyson might suitably enough have had the marriage of Parzival and Condiuiramur in mind when writing the Prince's aspiration. "Then reign the world's great bridals chaste and calm." Such passages in Wolfram's poem as Book iv. from line 666 and Book v. 676-682 may be commended to the critics who see nothing in mediæval love that is pure or faithful in the modern sense of marriage.

[13] *Petri Abælardi Historia Calamitatum. Petri Abælardi et Heloissæ Epistolæ.*

[14] *Bilder aus der deutschen Vergangenheit*, iii., 14-34.